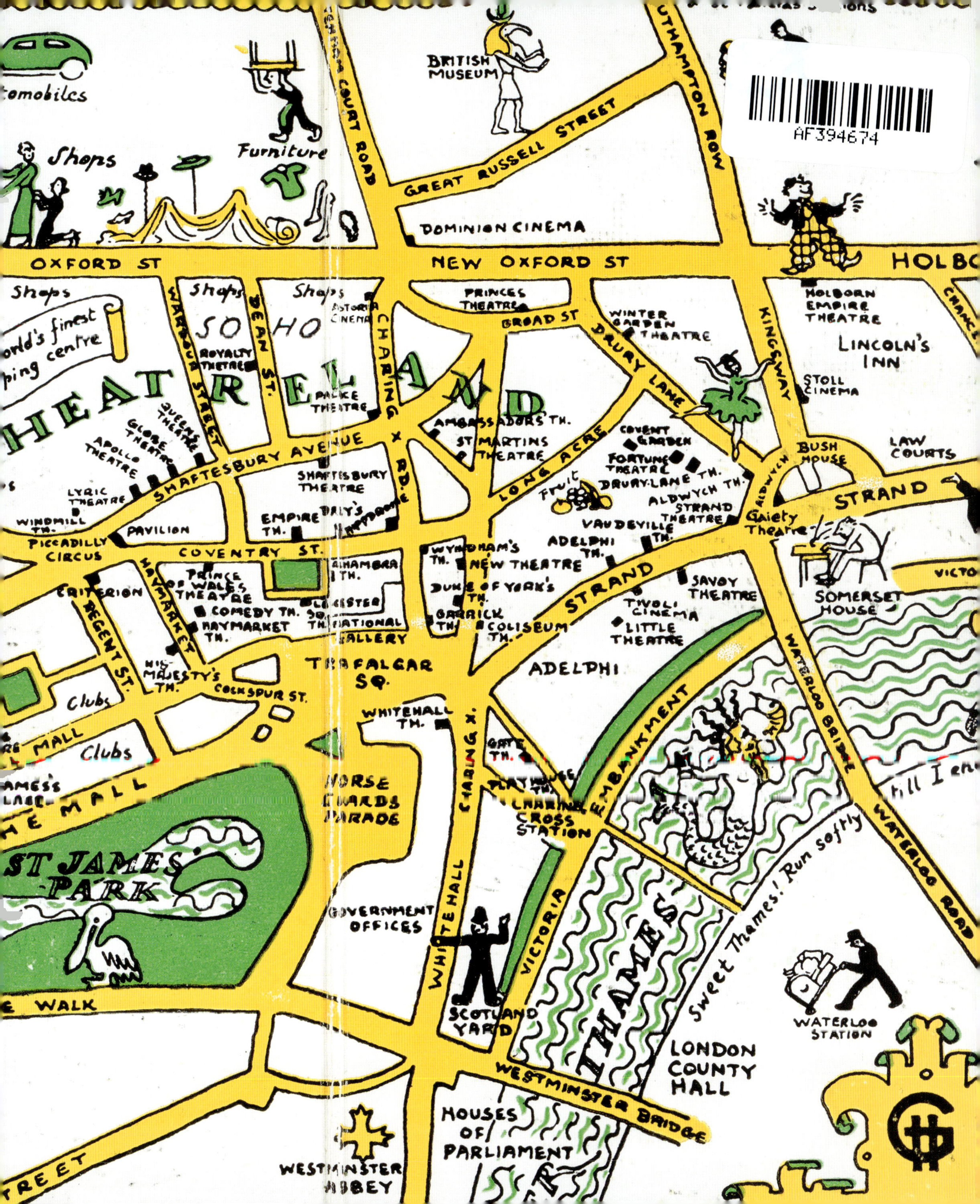

Automobiles
Shops
Furniture
BRITISH MUSEUM
GREAT RUSSELL STREET
TOTTENHAM COURT ROAD
SOUTHAMPTON ROW
DOMINION CINEMA
AF394674
OXFORD ST
NEW OXFORD ST
HOLBO
Shops
World's finest shopping centre
SO HO
Shops
Shops
ASTORIA CINEMA
PRINCES THEATRE
BROAD ST
WINTER GARDEN THEATRE
HOLBORN EMPIRE THEATRE
CHANC
WARDOUR STREET
DEAN ST.
CHARING CROSS ROAD
ROYALTY THEATRE
PALACE THEATRE
DRURY LANE
LINCOLN'S INN
STOLL CINEMA
THEATRELAND
QUEENS THEATRE
GLOBE THEATRE
AMBASSADORS TH.
ST MARTINS THEATRE
LONG ACRE
COVENT GARDEN
LAW COURTS
APOLLO THEATRE
SHAFTESBURY AVENUE
FORTUNE THEATRE
BUSH HOUSE
LYRIC THEATRE
SHAFTESBURY THEATRE
FRUIT
DRURY LANE TH.
ALDWYCH THEATRE
STRAND
WINDMILL TH.
EMPIRE TH.
DALY'S
HIPPODROME
VAUDEVILLE TH.
STRAND THEATRE
GAIETY THEATRE
PAVILION
PICCADILLY CIRCUS
COVENTRY ST.
ALHAMBRA TH.
WYNDHAM'S TH.
ADELPHI TH.
NEW THEATRE
VICTO
CRITERION
SACKVILLE STREET
PRINCE OF WALES THEATRE
LEICESTER SQ.
DUKE OF YORK'S TH.
SAVOY THEATRE
SOMERSET HOUSE
REGENT STREET
HAYMARKET
COMEDY TH.
HAYMARKET TH.
NATIONAL GALLERY
GARRICK TH.
COLISEUM TH.
TIVOLI CINEMA
LITTLE THEATRE
WATERLOO BRIDGE
HIS MAJESTY'S TH.
COCKSPUR ST.
TRAFALGAR SQ.
ADELPHI
Clubs
Clubs
WHITEHALL TH.
EMBANKMENT
THE MALL
HORSE GUARDS PARADE
GATE TH.
PLAYHOUSE TH.
CHARING CROSS STATION
hill I en
ST JAMES'S PALACE
CHARING X.
WHITEHALL
ST JAMES'S PARK
GOVERNMENT OFFICES
VICTORIA
THAMES
Sweet Thames! Run softly
WATERLOO ROAD
THE WALK
SCOTLAND YARD
WATERLOO STATION
LONDON COUNTY HALL
WESTMINSTER BRIDGE
STREET
HOUSES OF PARLIAMENT
WESTMINSTER ABBEY

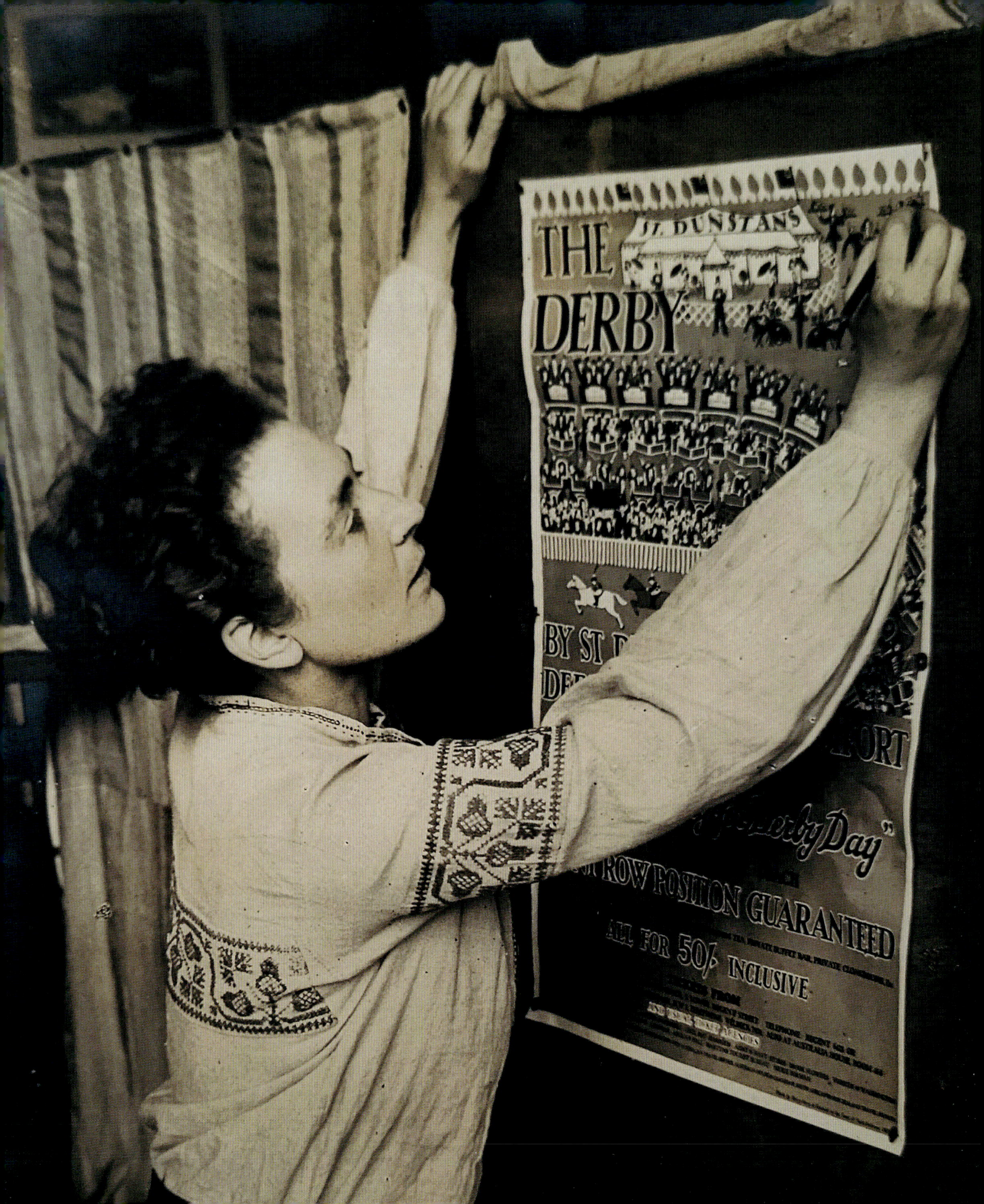
ST. DUNSTANS
THE
DERBY
BY ST D
DERB
ORT
"Derby Day"
ROW POSITION GUARANTEED
ALL FOR 50/- INCLUSIVE

HERRY PERRY
ARTIST & ILLUSTRATOR

A Biography by Julian Francis

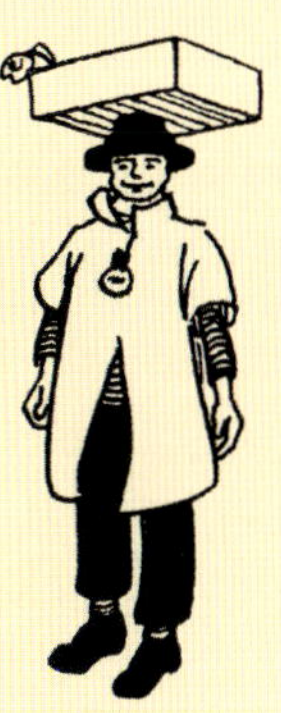

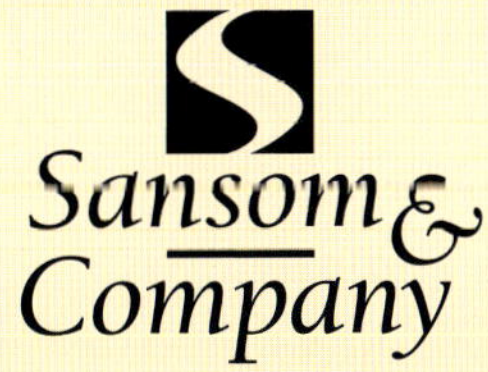

Sansom &
Company

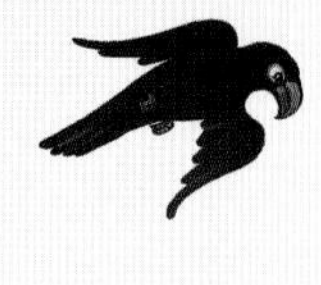
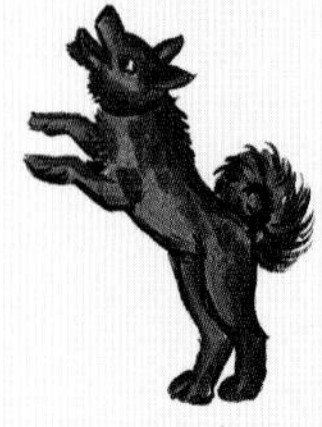

To my children:
Celia, Guy and Hope.

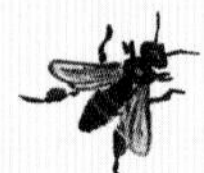

First published in 2024 by Sansom and Company,
a publishing imprint of Redcliffe Press Ltd., 81g Pembroke Road, Bristol BS8 3EA
www.sansomandcompany.co.uk | info@sansomandcompany.co.uk

ISBN 978-1-915670-17-5

Every effort has been made to trace any relevant copyright holders and obtain permission to reproduce the material in this book. Please do get in touch with any enquiries or information relating to material reproduced here or to the rights holder/s.

British Library Cataloguing-in-Publication Data
A catalogue record for this book is available from the British Library. All rights reserved.

Edited by Ann Kay
Design and typesetting by Richard Keenan at Design Now
Printed and bound by Akcent Media

Front cover: redrawn and adapted from a letterhead designed by Herry Perry
Rear cover: the preparatory drawing for The Good Neighbour pub sign, 1950s
Inside cover: detail of the map for the Grosvenor House hotel, Park Lane, London, c.1936
Frontispiece: Herry Perry holding a copy of her Derby Day poster for St Dunstan's, 1929

CONTENTS

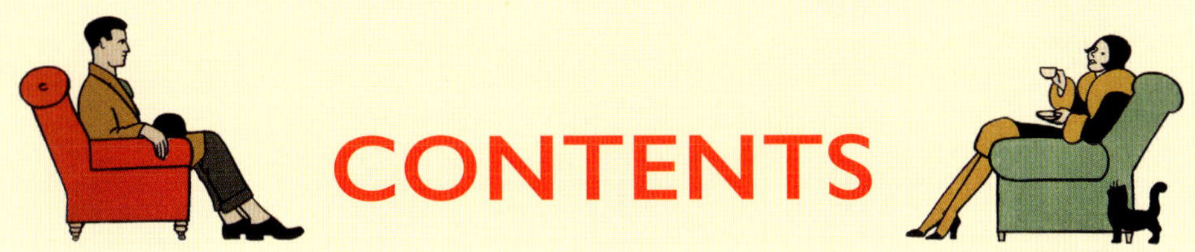

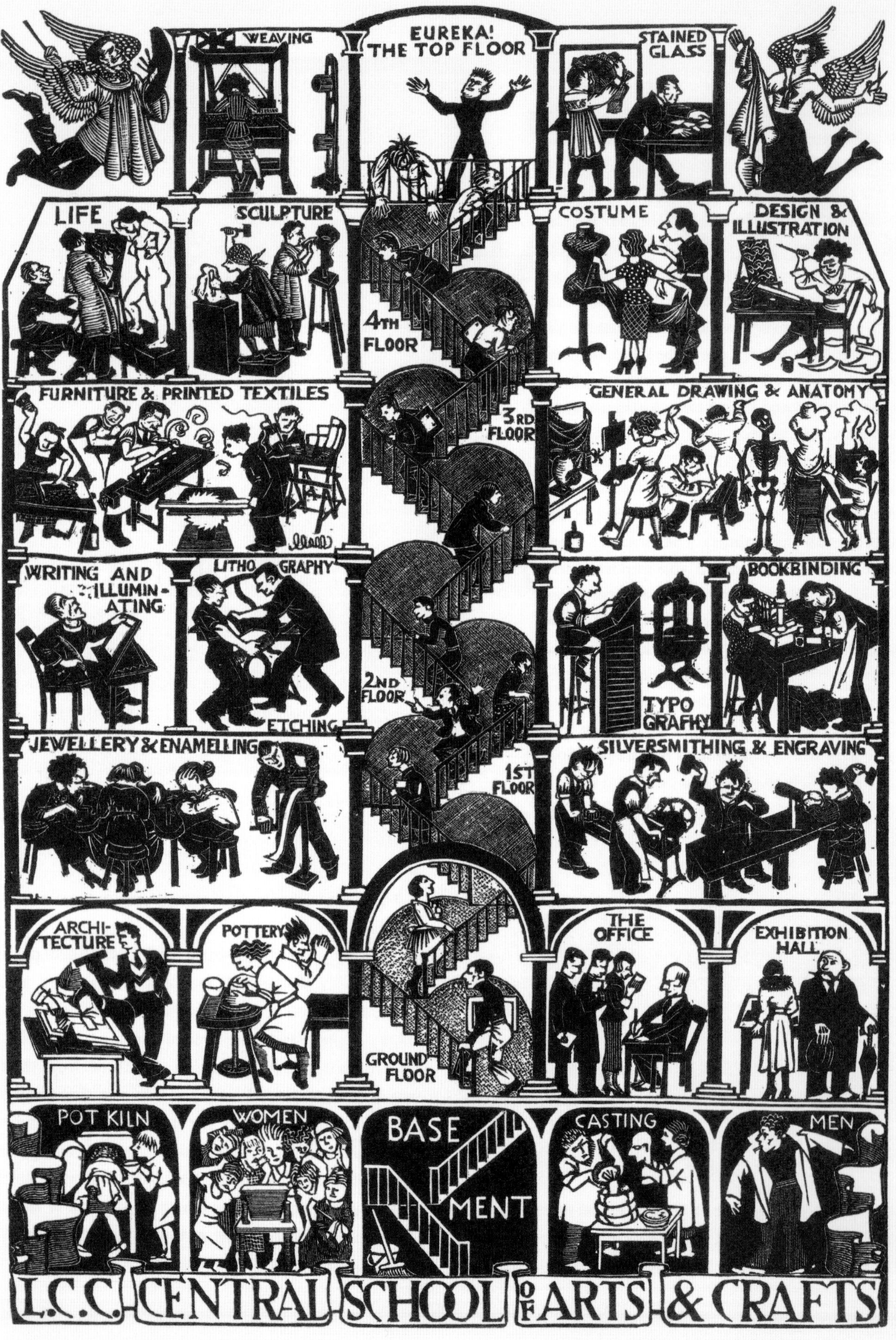

WEAVING
EUREKA! THE TOP FLOOR
STAINED GLASS
LIFE
SCULPTURE
4TH FLOOR
COSTUME
DESIGN & ILLUSTRATION
FURNITURE & PRINTED TEXTILES
3RD FLOOR
GENERAL DRAWING & ANATOMY
WRITING AND ILLUMINATING
LITHO GRAPHY
2ND FLOOR
TYPO GRAPHY
BOOKBINDING
ETCHING
JEWELLERY & ENAMELLING
1ST FLOOR
SILVERSMITHING & ENGRAVING
ARCHI- TECTURE
POTTERY
GROUND FLOOR
THE OFFICE
EXHIBITION HALL
POT KILN
WOMEN
BASE MENT
CASTING
MEN
L.C.C. CENTRAL SCHOOL OF ARTS & CRAFTS

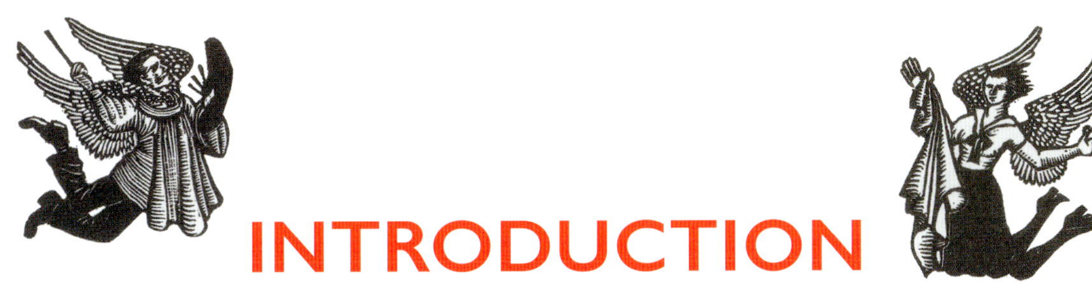

INTRODUCTION

I had not heard of Herry Perry until I went to an exhibition by Angie Lewin in Winchester in 2017. This included artwork by other artists who had influenced her, and there was a wood engraving by Herry Perry. It was a witty cross-section of the Central School of Arts and Crafts (now Central Saint Martins) in the 1920s. I wanted to find out more about her but information seemed to be very thin on the ground. None of the leading books on wood engraving mentioned her, and it wasn't until I found a 6 May 2017 blog by Rod Barron of Barron Maps that I began to learn anything about her. This blog also introduced me to her posters and maps. Following a conversation with Simon Lawrence of the Fleece Press I was put in touch with Herry Perry's nieces, who still had artwork by her as well as lots of information about her life and art.

This book brings together almost all of Herry Perry's artwork and allows us to make a full assessment of this witty and versatile artist for the first time. It will hopefully bring her out of obscurity so that she can be recognised as an important artist of the 1920s–50s.

Opposite: *L.C.C. Central School of Arts and Crafts*, wood engraving, late 1920s, 520 x 375 mm (courtesy of the CSM Museum and Collections)

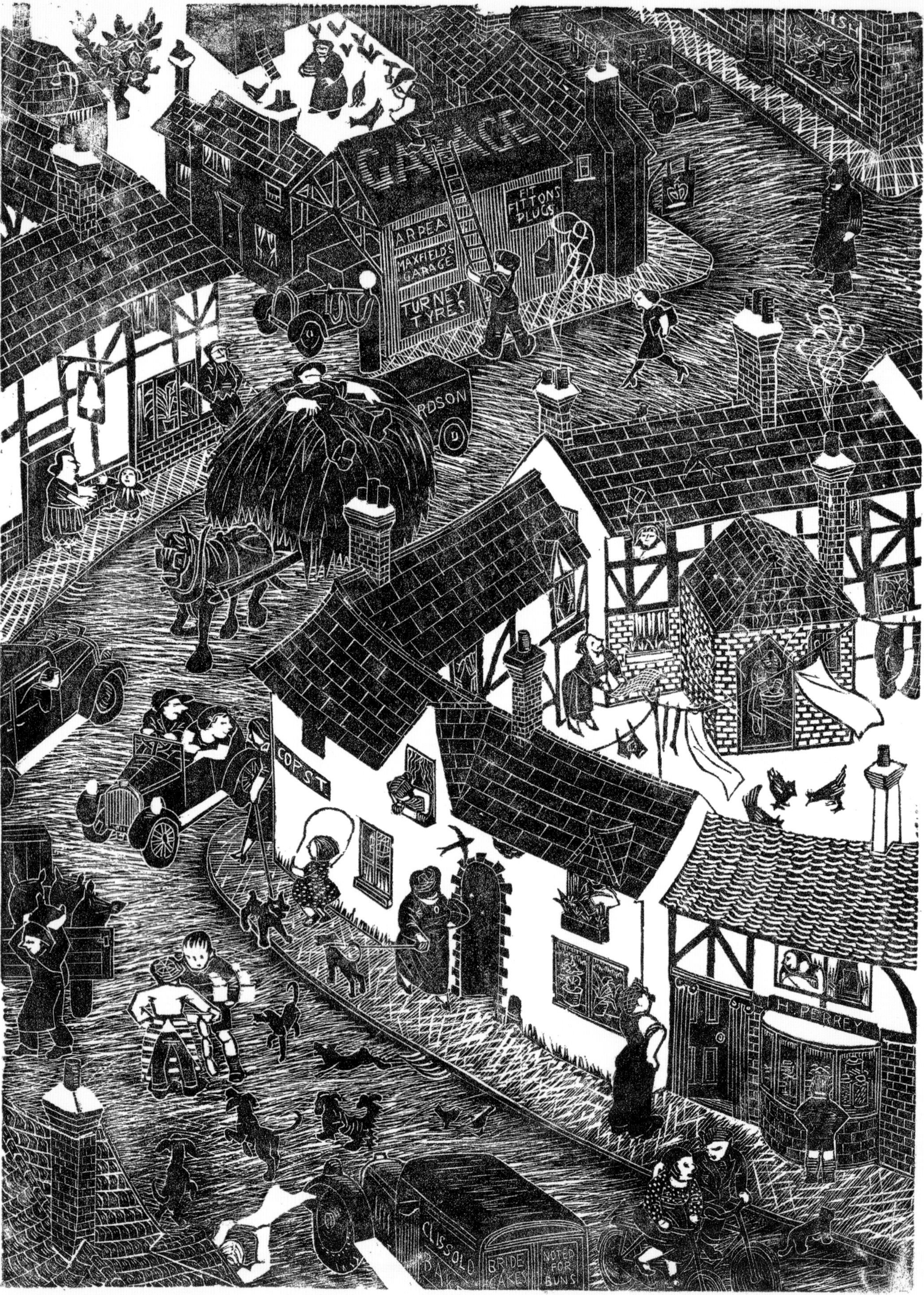
GARAGE
AR PEA
MAXFIELDS
GARAGE
TURNEY
TYRES
FIT FITTONS
PLUGS
PDSON
COP ST
PERREY
CLISSOLD
BRIDE
CAKES
NOTED FOR
BUNS

BRIEF BIOGRAPHY

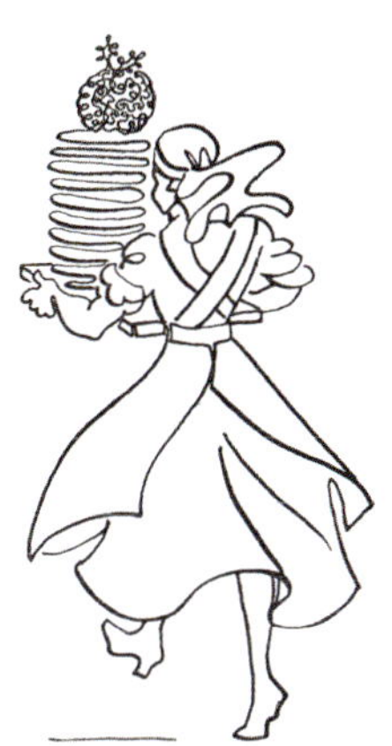

Herry Perry was born near Bolton in 1897 into a wealthy family. She was christened Anne Erica Thackeray but disliked those names and was known as Heather (*Erica* is the Latin for the heather plant), which was then shortened to Herry, presumably for the obvious reason that the rhyme with her surname was catchy. She sometimes signed her work Herry-Perry. Her father Ottley Perry (1845–1924) was a cotton merchant and a significant figure in Bolton politics and the local militia. He designed the first coat of arms for the County Borough of Bolton, constituted in 1890, and this may have sparked Herry's interest in heraldry (see the 'Pub Signs' section).

The family moved south in around 1900, first to Kensington in London and then to Northwood in Middlesex. Herry's sister Rosamund was born in 1902. Both the daughters attended St Helen's School, which was adjacent to the family house in Northwood (and they may also have been home-schooled at certain stages). Herry wanted to attend art school but her father was very much against the idea, so initially

Opposite: *Safety First – High Street, Ellesmote*, wood engraving, early 1930s and exhibited in 1931, 290 x 205 mm (courtesy of the CSM Museum and Collections)

she worked as a secretary to a Member of Parliament. But, following her father's death in 1924, she finally went to the Central School of Arts and Crafts for three years. Little is known about her time there but she appears to have been a friend of Central student Joyce Clissold (1905–1982), whose name appears on the side of a van in the wood engraving *Safety First – High Street, Ellesmote* (see page 8). Clissold went on to be a successful textile designer and producer with shops in central London, and she may have been supplied with designs by Herry, who herself designed fabrics. Herry would have been taught wood engraving, and a broad range of other arts and crafts, by Noel Rooke (1881–1953). Head of the School of Book Production at Central from 1914 to 1946 and a very influential teacher, he was also crucial to the development of wood engraving in the 1920s and '30s. He was a member of the Society of Wood Engravers (SWE), which he co-founded in 1920.

Herry's artistic career is dealt with in the sections below. As for other aspects of her life, during the Second World War she worked as a Voluntary Aid Detachment nurse. At least part of her time as a VAD was at the Military Hospital, Shenley, Hertfordshire, and thereafter she took part in first-aid work as a member of St John Ambulance. She co-wrote a first-aid book in 1940 (see the 'Book Illustration' section).

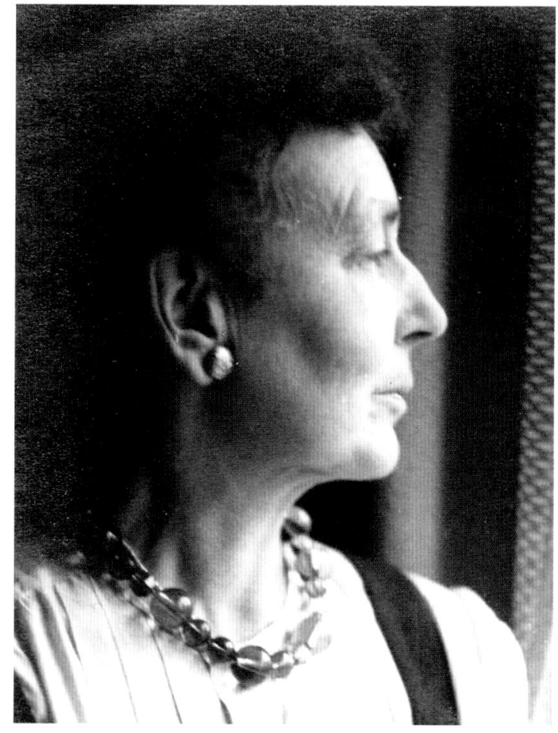

Above: Herry Perry, 1930/40s
Below: Herry Perry, 1950s

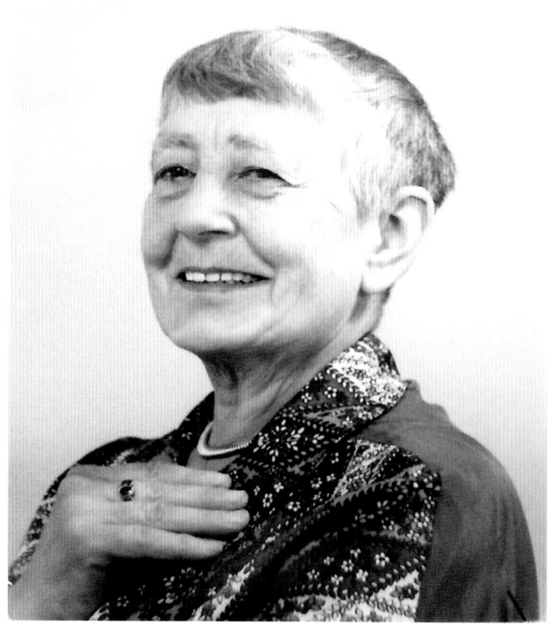

Below: [untitled portrait of a young woman engraving a boxwood block], linocut, 1924-7, 80 x 115 mm

Herry never married and died in 1962. Her short obituary in *The Times*, on 11 September 1962, described her as a 'loyal, colourful and generous friend' and 'much more than a talented commercial artist'. Her nieces remember her as a bohemian with a distinctive dress sense who was fiercely independent but also a warm person with a lovely sense of humour and a very observant eye.

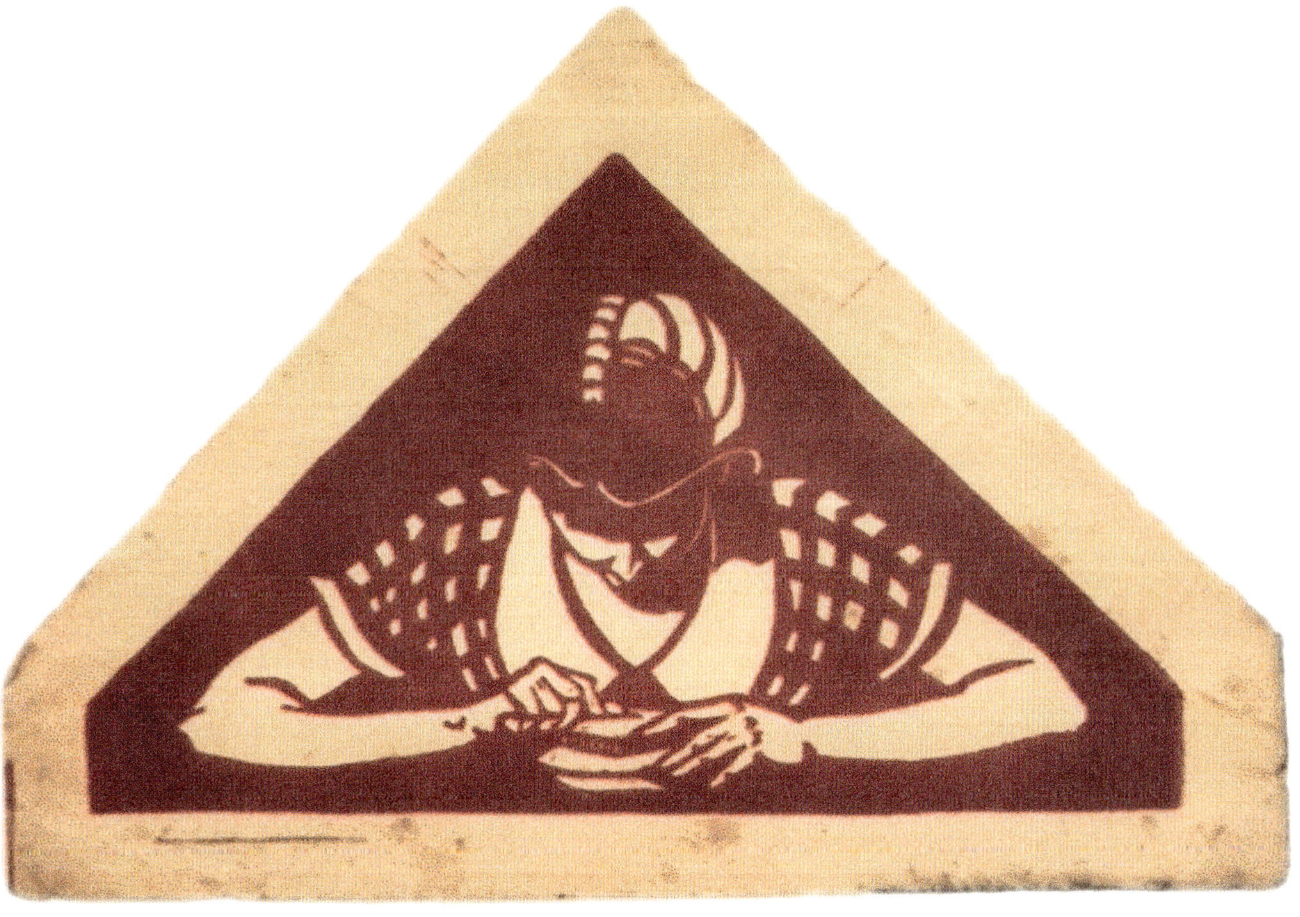

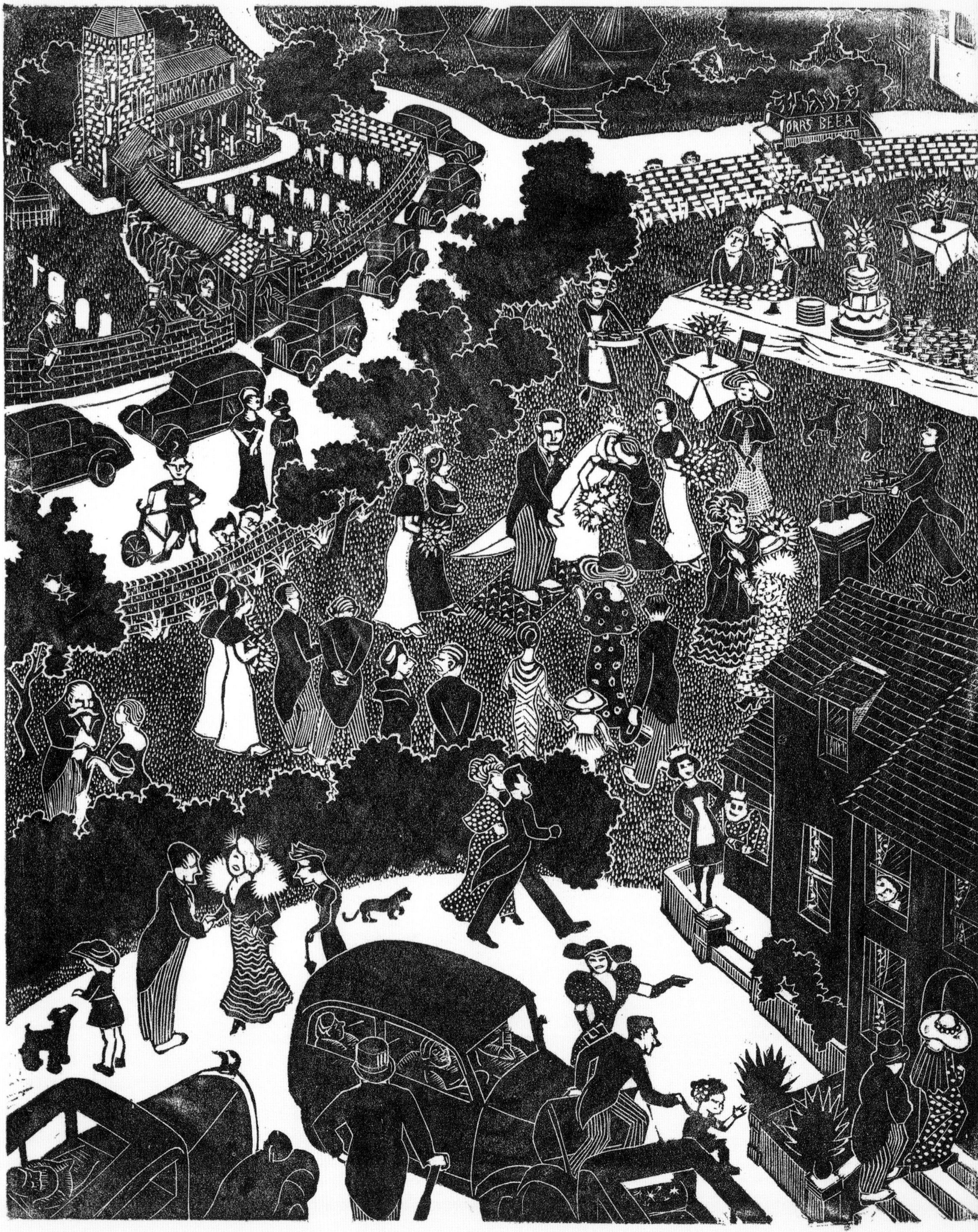
ORRS BEER

WOOD ENGRAVING, SCULPTURE and 'STUPID LITTLE JOBS'

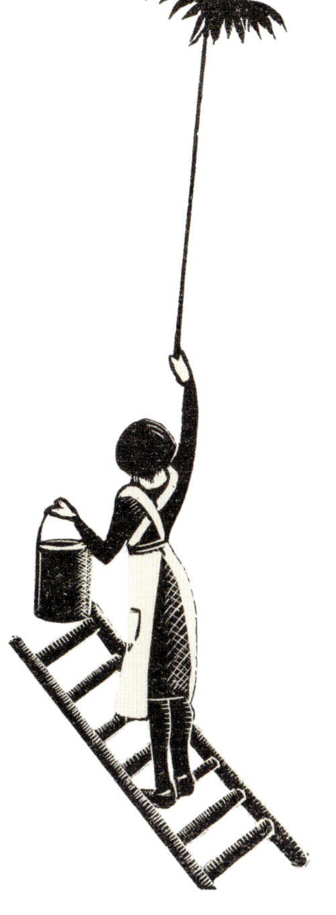

Like most other artists, Herry had to earn a living – and not always in ways that she particularly liked. When writing to Sir John Russell (see the 'Murals' section) on 7 July 1932, she said:

At the present moment I am doing a variety of stupid little jobs – Christmas cards (of all things) & designs for wine labels, playing cards & the outsides of crime novels.

Her first love was wood engraving. It's difficult to date her wood engravings because she didn't date them herself and there is little other information about them. However, they were probably all produced in the period 1924–32. She certainly exhibited *Safety First – High Street*, *Ellesmote* and *Billingsgate Bloke* in 1931 and *Wedding at Ellesmote* in 1932. Although she exhibited with the Society of Wood Engravers and the English Wood Engraving Society, she was never a member of either organisation.

There are a number of her wood engravings in the archives of Central Saint Martins and *Safety*

Opposite: *Wedding at Ellesmote,* wood engraving, early 1930s and exhibited in 1932, 260 x 205 mm (courtesy of the Science Museum, Science and Society Picture Library)

First – High Street, Ellesmote and *Wedding at Ellesmote* are in the Science Museum Group's Science & Society Picture Library. *Wedding at Ellesmote* shows a crowded wedding reception in a garden with some amusing vignettes including the boys on the church wall looking at the cars and guests arriving. *Safety First – High Street, Ellesmote* is a wittily playful scene of a chaotic street where Herry has put her name above one of the shops (with her surname spelled Perrey, for some unknown reason) and her friend Joyce Clissold's name on the side of one of the vans. She also did three portraits – *Billingsgate Bloke*, *Mrs Budgett* and another of a young man – of which *Mrs Budgett* is the best. These three small wood engravings all date from her time at the Central School of Arts and Crafts (1924–7). By far the best wood engraving is her cross-section of the Central showing all its various departments, including a crowd of women in the basement lavatory fighting over the mirror (see page 6 for the full image).

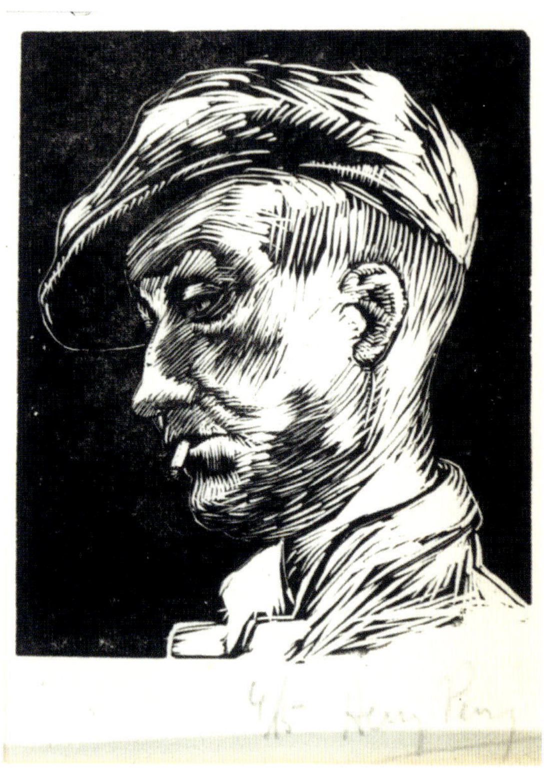

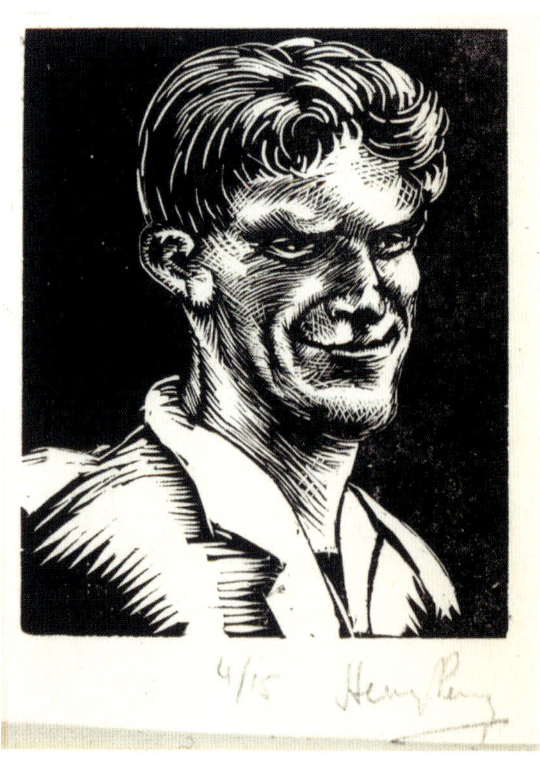

Right top: *Billingsgate Bloke*, wood engraving (4/15), 1924-7, 75 x 60 mm (courtesy of the CSM Museum and Collections)

Right bottom: [untitled portrait of a young man], wood engraving (4/15), 1924-7, 75 x 60 mm (courtesy of the CSM Museum and Collections)

Opposite top: *Mrs Budgett,* wood engraving, 1924-7, 58 x 50 mm (courtesy of the CSM Museum and Collections)

Opposite bottom: *L.C.C. Central School of Arts and Crafts* (detail), wood engraving, late 1920s, 520 x 375 mm (courtesy of the CSM Museum and Collections)

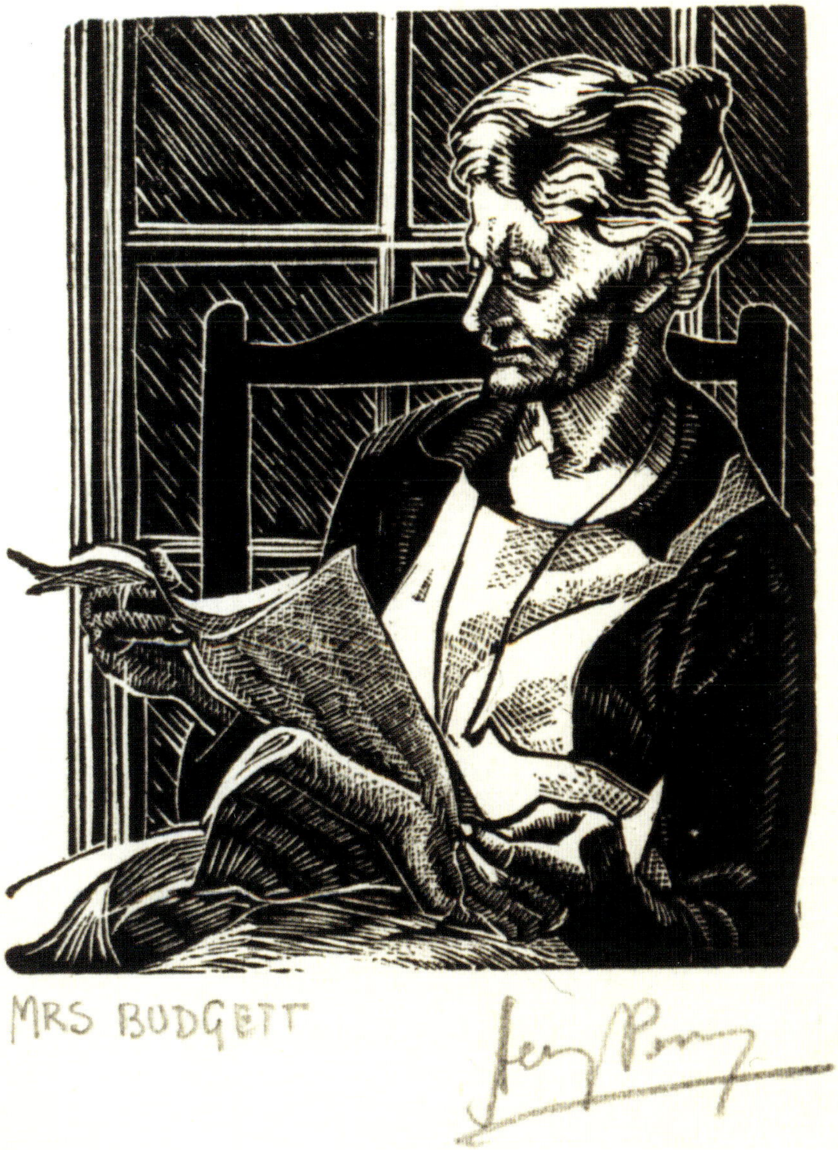

MRS BUDGETT

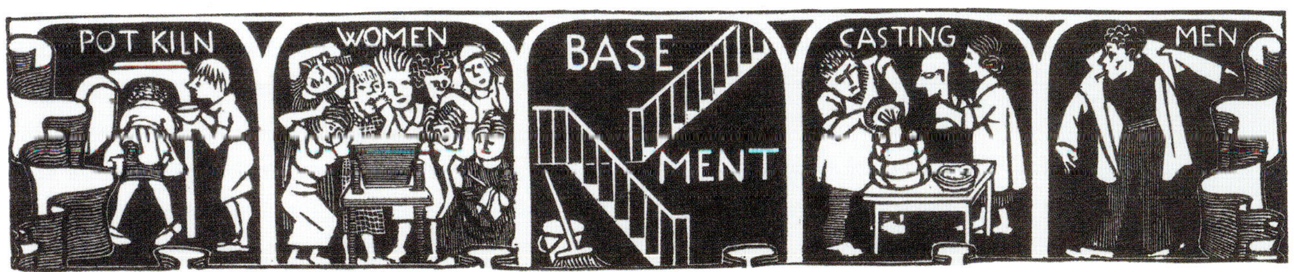

Despite her misgivings, Herry did do a number of excellent Christmas cards in the 1930s and '40s featuring wood engravings, for herself and her mother. She also designed Christmas cards for other people (such as Rothamsted Experimental Station, see the 'Murals' section), either with wood engravings or linocuts. This was a common practice then, and artists would print them with the client's address and a message if the client wanted that. Note, in the Christmas linocuts, the appearance of animals, which she liked drawing – including a male giraffe smoking a cigar! Herry designed playing cards, too. One design was for her sister Rosamund and Rosamund's husband Roger Shaen, a Scottish lawyer (see page 21).

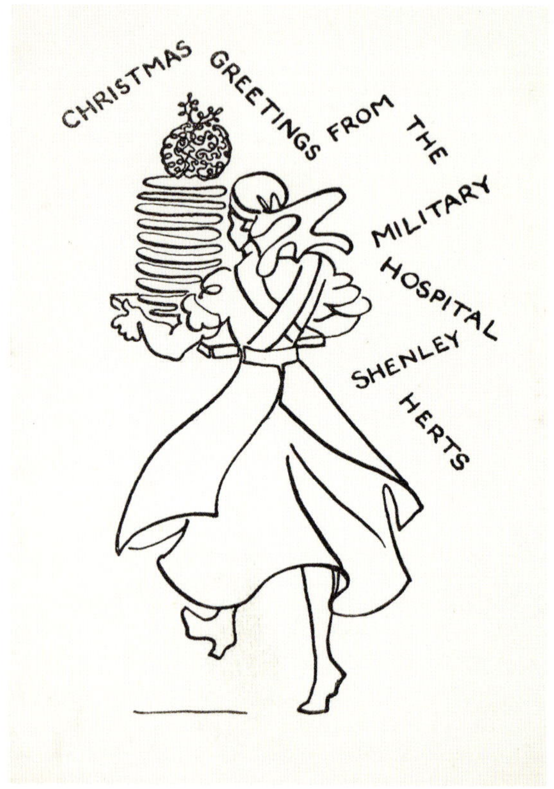

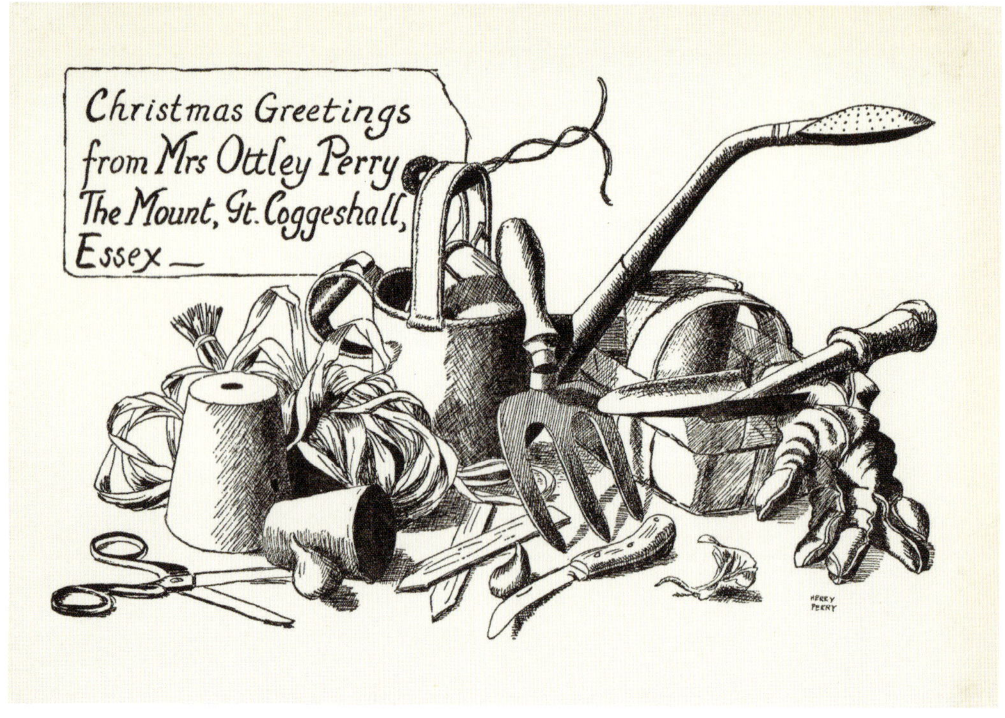

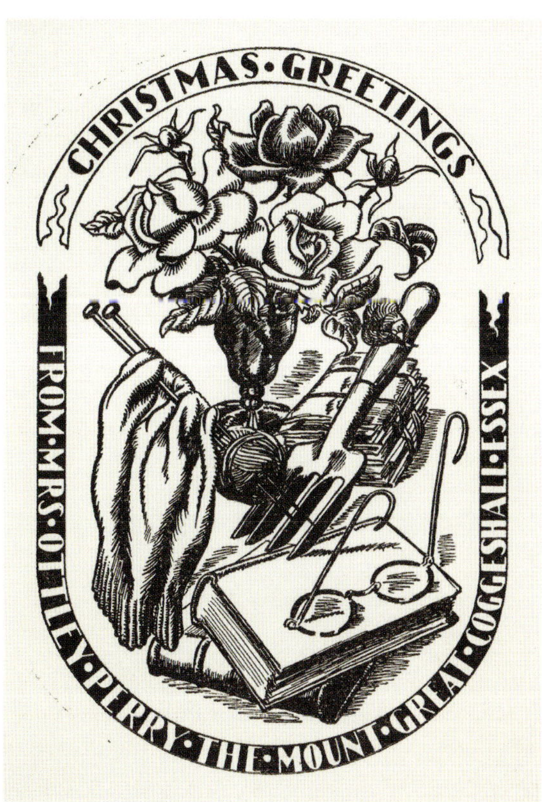

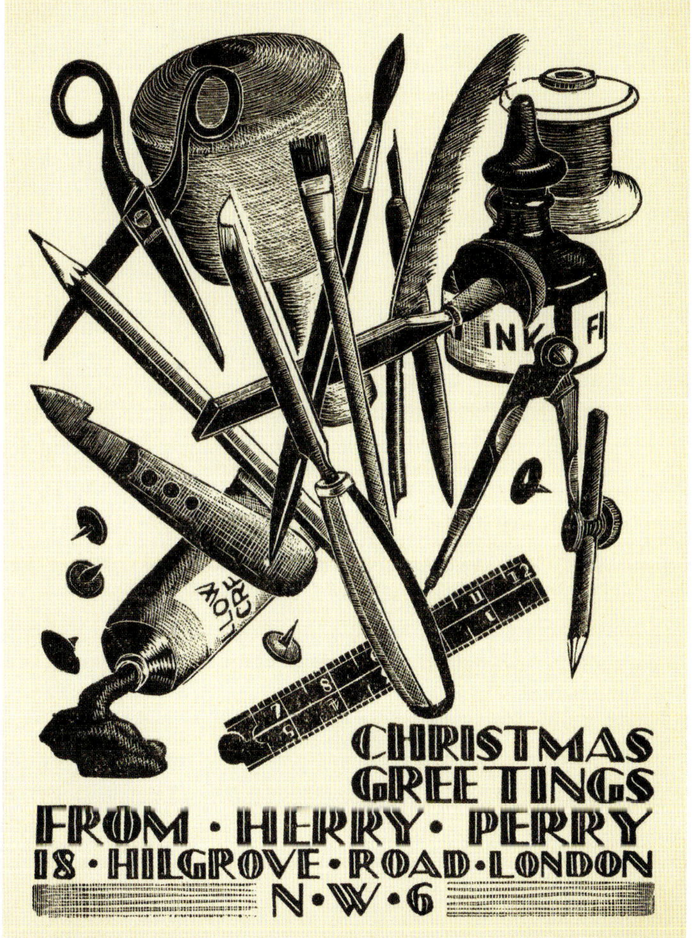

Above, right and opposite: Christmas cards, wood engravings, 1935-1940

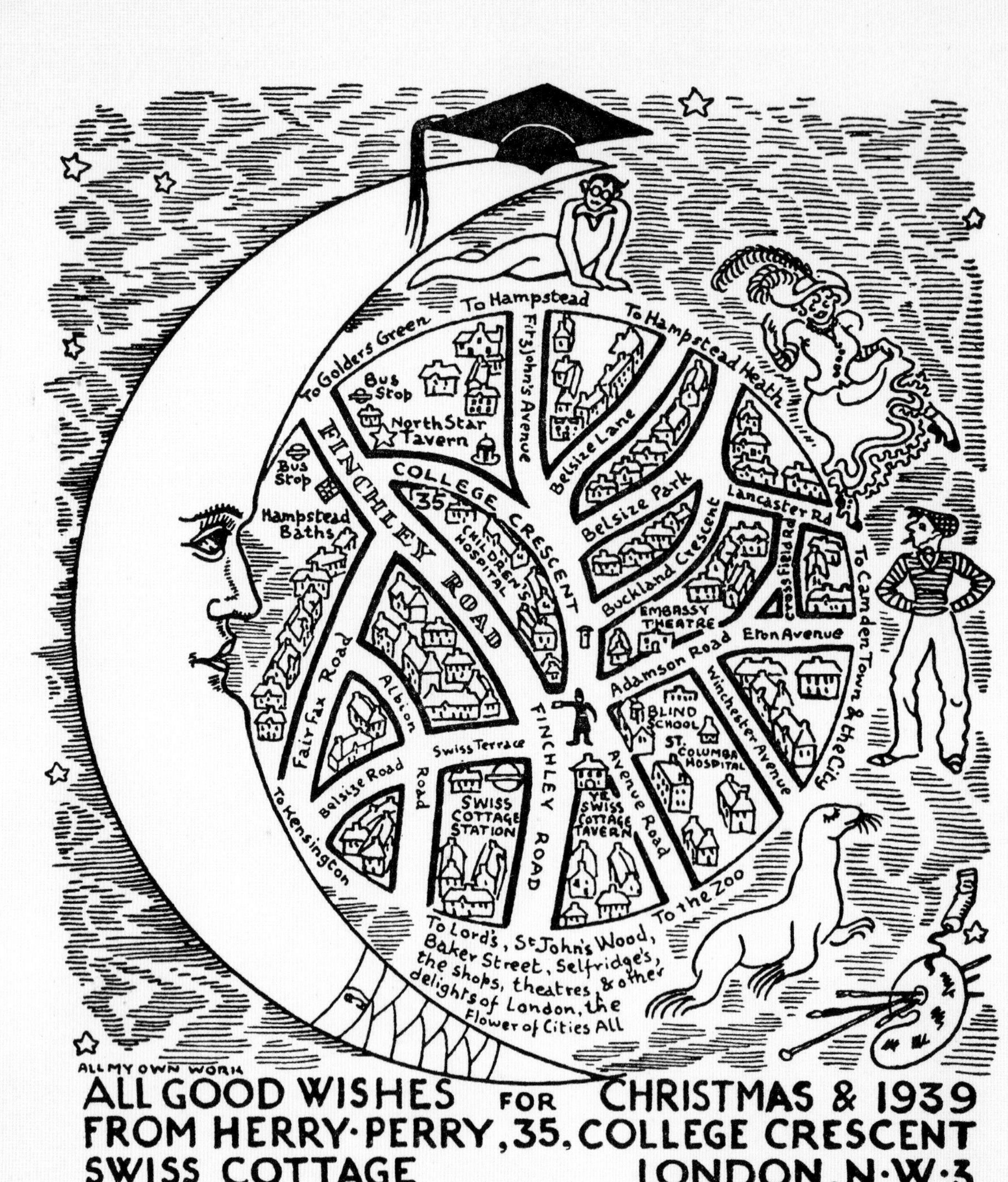
To Golders Green
To Hampstead
To Hampstead Heath
Fitzjohn's Avenue
Belsize Lane
Bus Stop
North Star Tavern
FINCHLEY ROAD
COLLEGE CRESCENT
Belsize Park
Lancaster Rd
Bus Stop
35
CHILDREN'S HOSPITAL
Buckland Crescent
Crossfield Road
To Camden Town & the City
Hampstead Baths
EMBASSY THEATRE
Fairfax Road
Albion Road
Adamson Road
Eton Avenue
Winchester Avenue
BLIND SCHOOL
ST. COLUMBA HOSPITAL
FINCHLEY ROAD
Belsize Road
Swiss Terrace
SWISS COTTAGE STATION
YE SWISS COTTAGE TAVERN
Avenue Road
To Kensington
To the Zoo
To Lord's, St. John's Wood, Baker Street, Selfridge's, the shops, theatres & other delights of London, the Flower of Cities All
ALL MY OWN WORK
ALL GOOD WISHES FOR CHRISTMAS & 1939
FROM HERRY·PERRY, 35, COLLEGE CRESCENT
SWISS COTTAGE   LONDON, N·W·3

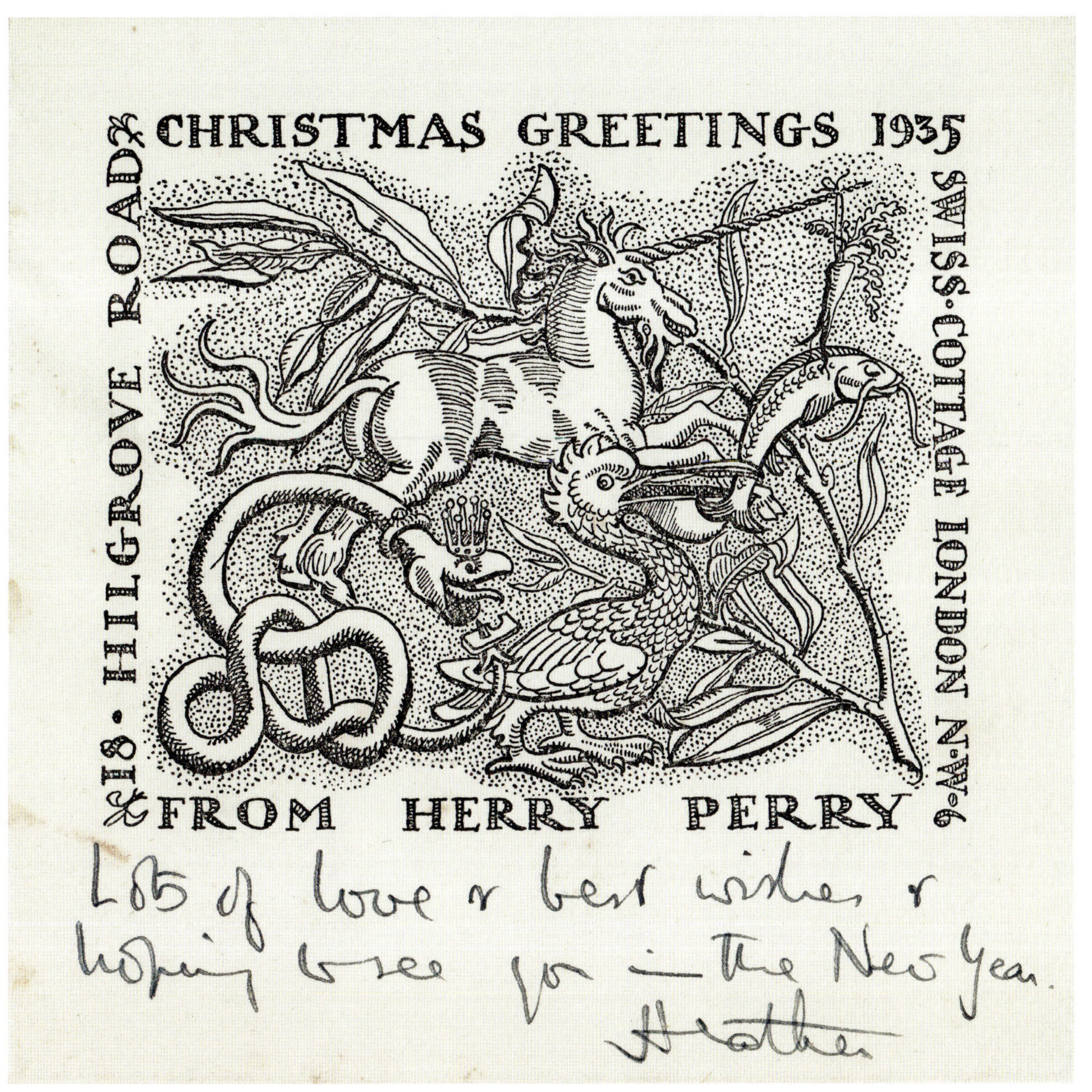

Above and opposite: Christmas cards, wood
engravings, various sizes, 1935-1940

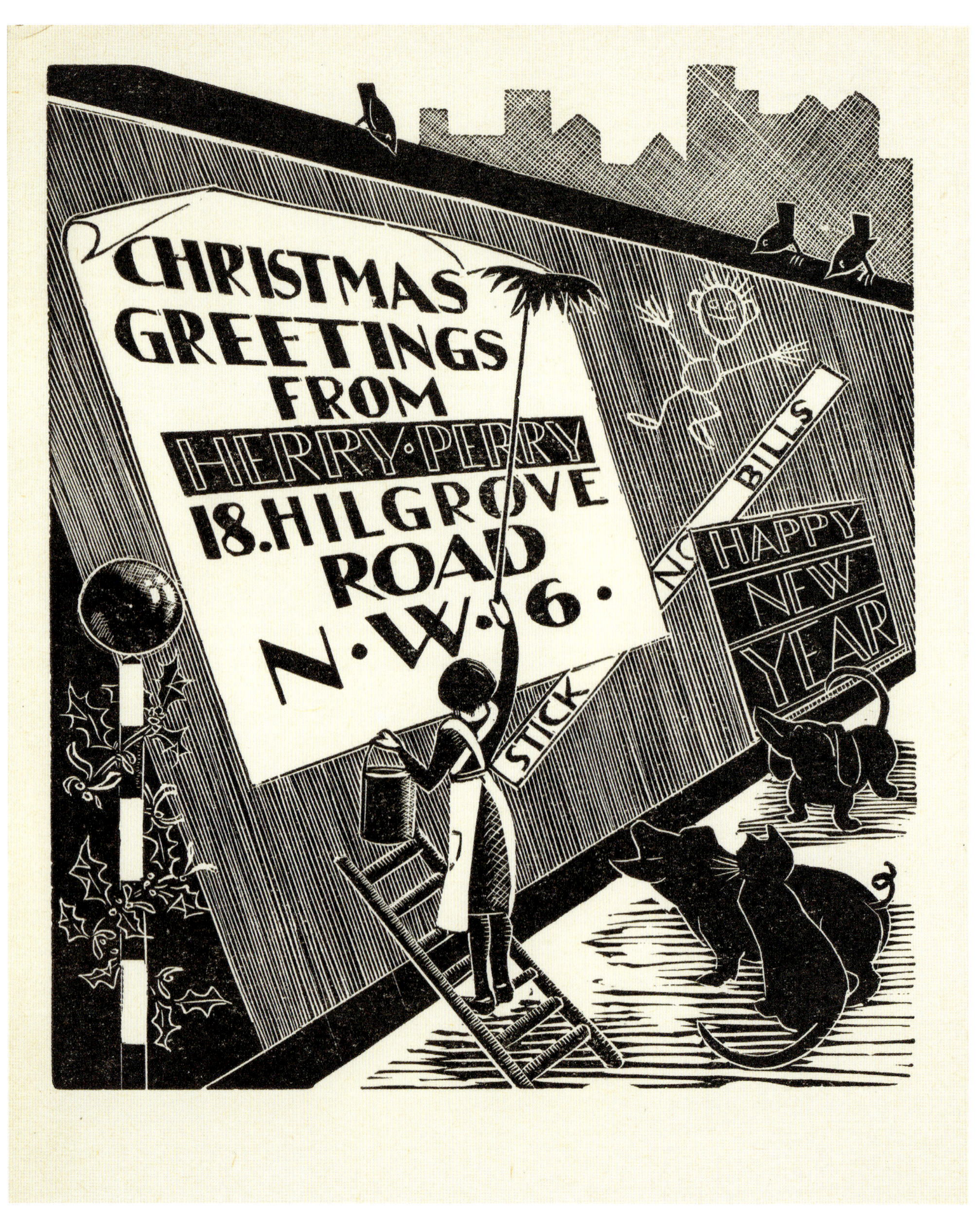
CHRISTMAS
GREETINGS
FROM
HERRY · PERRY
18. HILGROVE
ROAD
N. W. 6.
STICK
NO
BILLS
HAPPY
NEW
YEAR

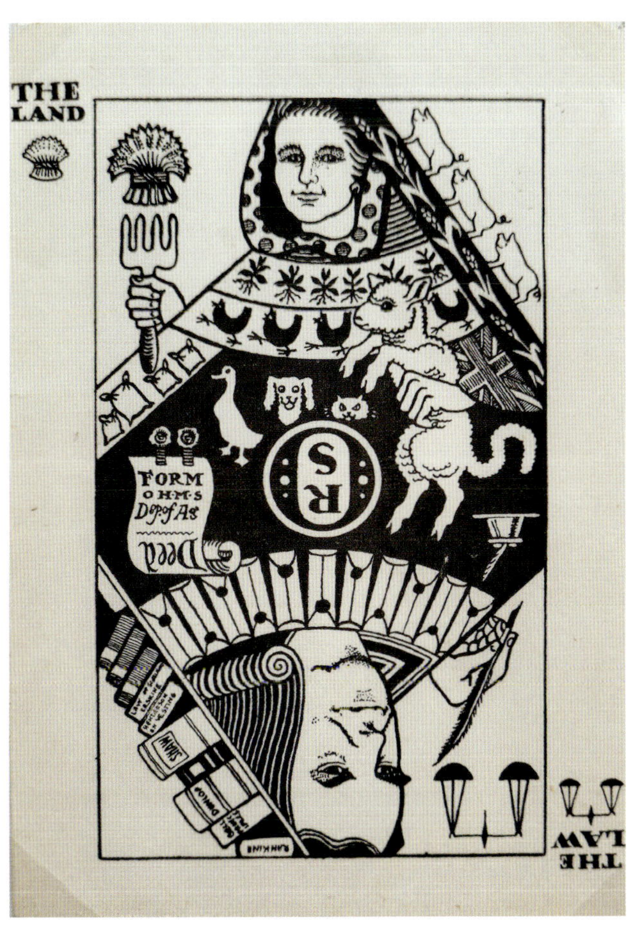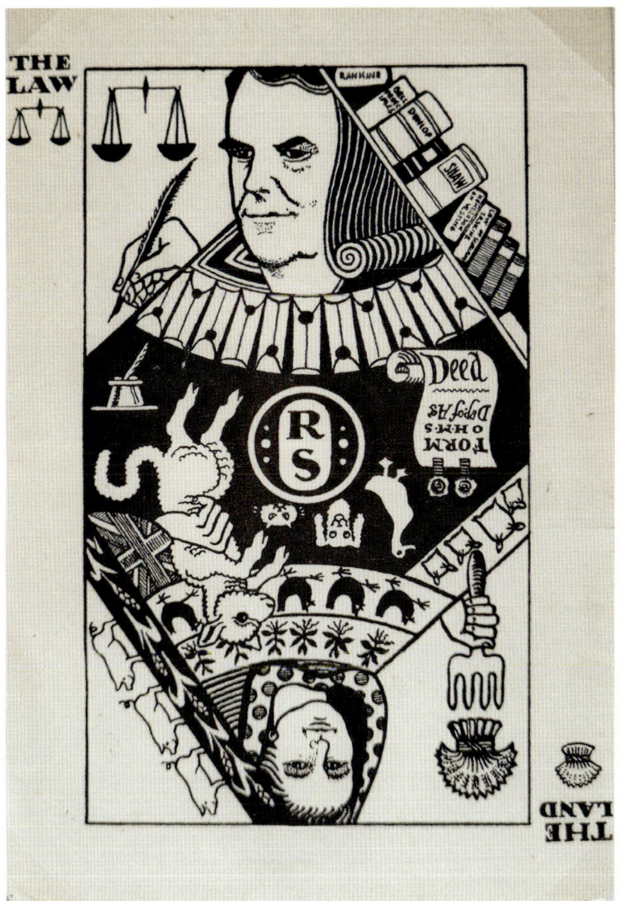

Above: Playing card, 1930s

Opposite: Christmas card, wood engraving, 1935-1940

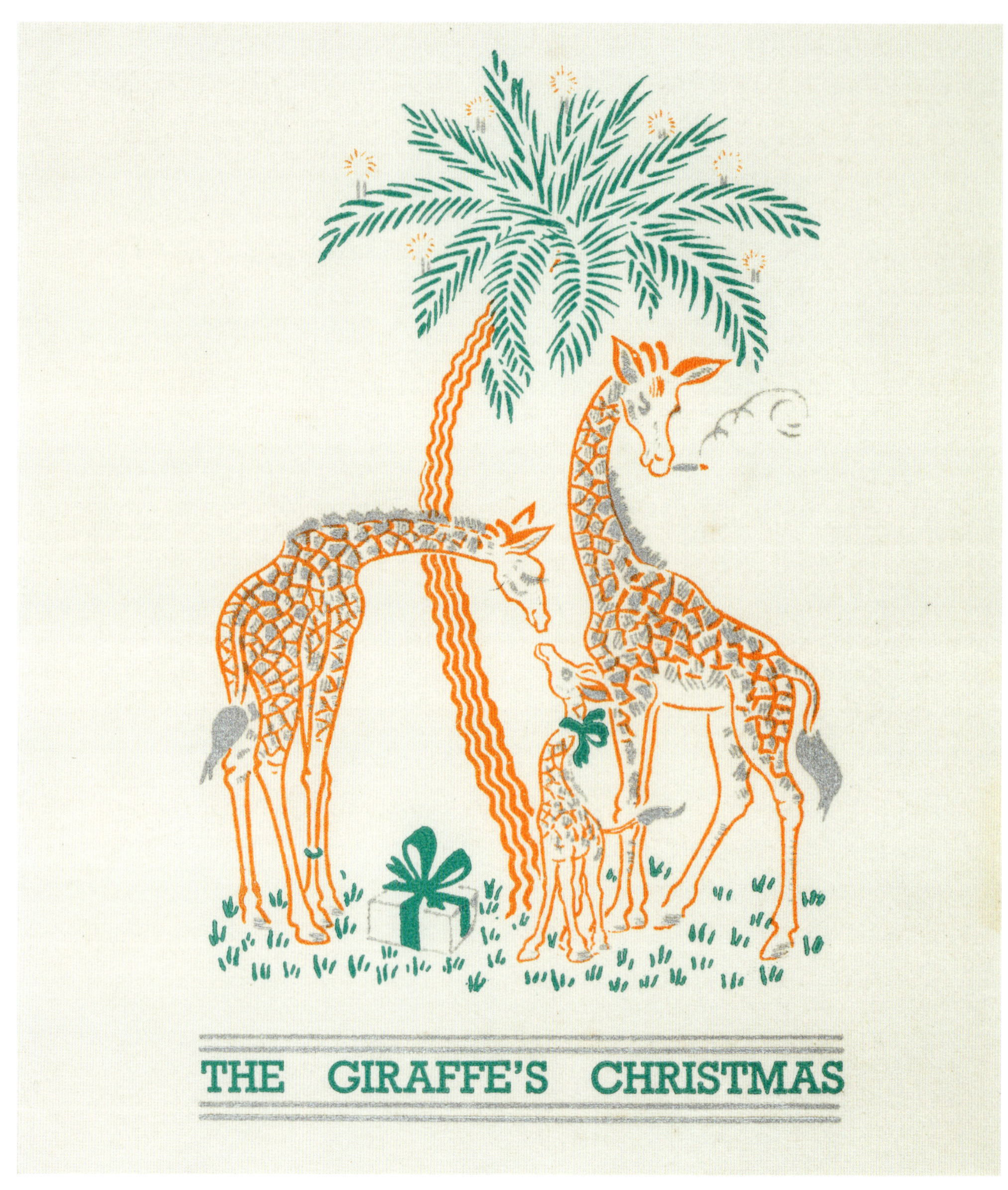

THE GIRAFFE'S CHRISTMAS

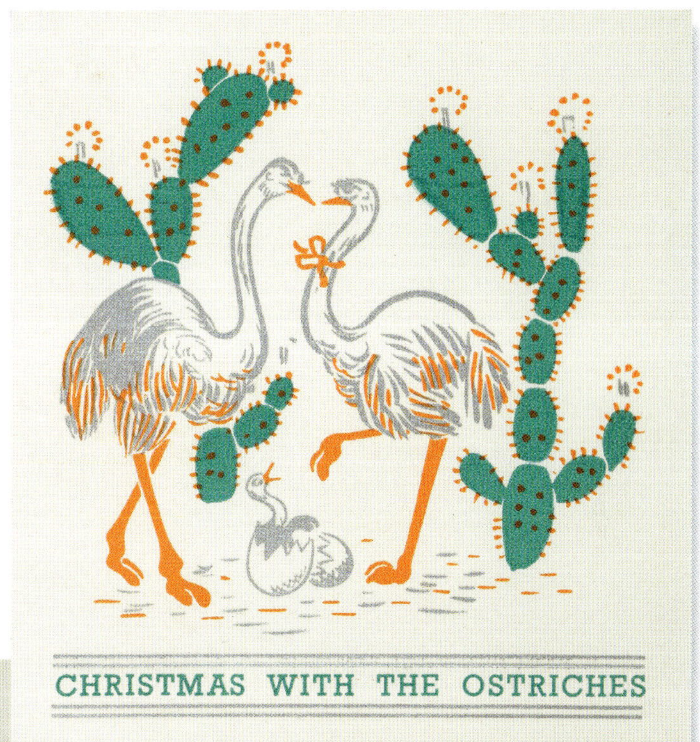

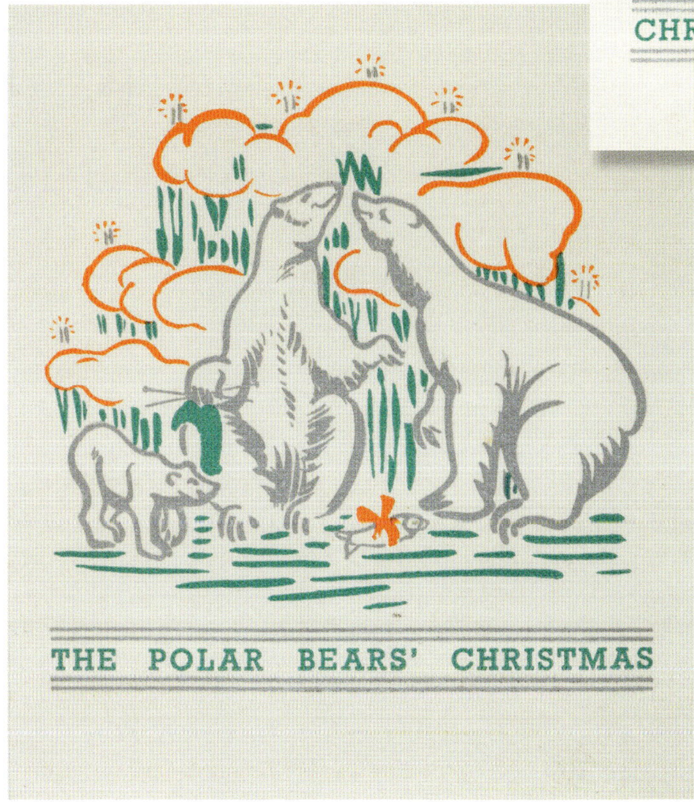

Above and opposite: Christmas cards, linocuts,
1930s, 140 x 115 mm

Herry was also a sculptor and we have photographs of three of her sculptures. Her most successful, in my opinion, is *The Mermaids' Marriage*, showing two entwined mermaids. There is a reference to her *Swinging Monkey* in the *Chelmsford Chronicle* of 8 October 1937, and also a photograph of a duck carved in wood. She exhibited a *Red Ike* carved lacewood doorstop (item 179) – shown in a surviving photograph of Herry with the sculpture – at the Arts and Crafts Exhibition Society in 1938 and also an elephant head in walnut (item 181). 'Red Ike' is probably a reference to a scene from the popular historical novel *Red Ike: A Novel of Cumberland* by J.M. Denwood and S. Fowler Wright, published in 1931 by Hutchinson.

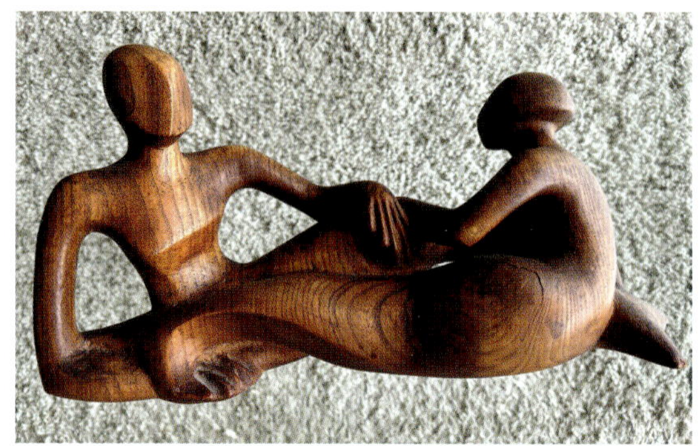

Above: *The Mermaids' Marriage*, sculpture in wood, 1930s

Below: Herry Perry with her *Red Ike* sculpture carved from lacewood, 1930s

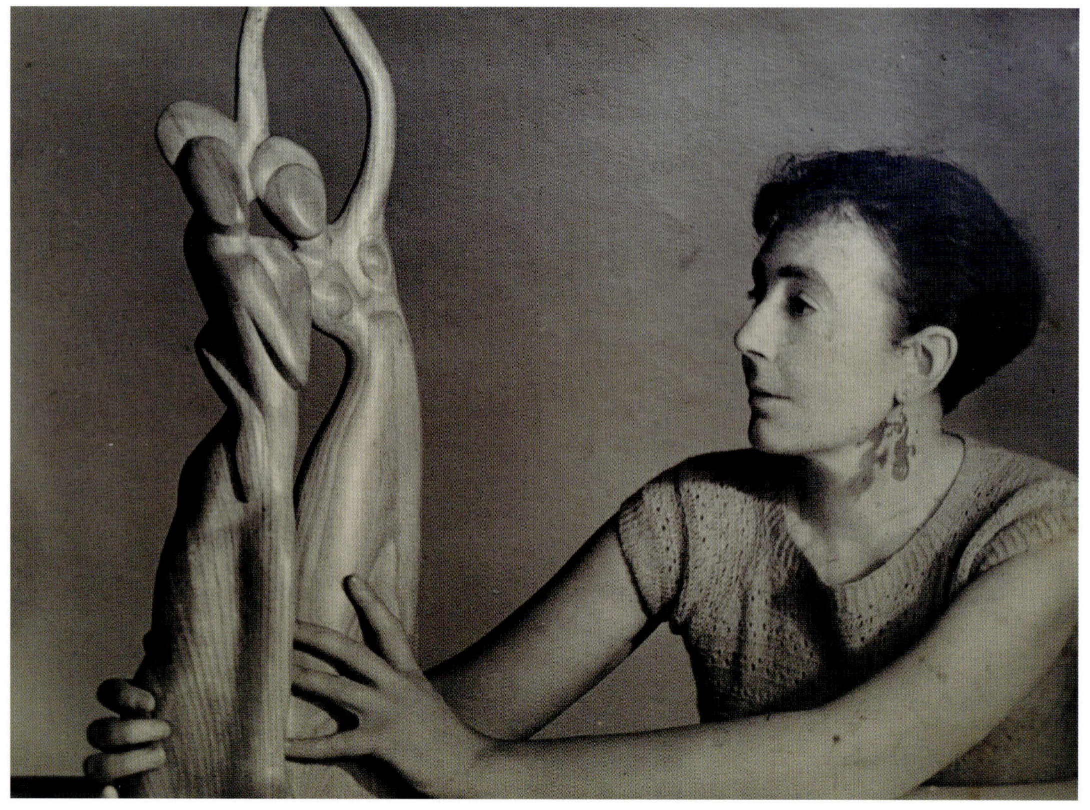

Herry was one of many artists who created designs for the Post Office's regular issues of new forms of Greetings Telegram. Her Greetings Telegram for St Valentine's Day 1939 was bright, colourful and full of posies.

Above: Post Office Greetings Telegram for St Valentine's Day 1939, 164 x 215 mm

Right and below: details of Post Office Greetings Telegram for St Valentine's Day 1939

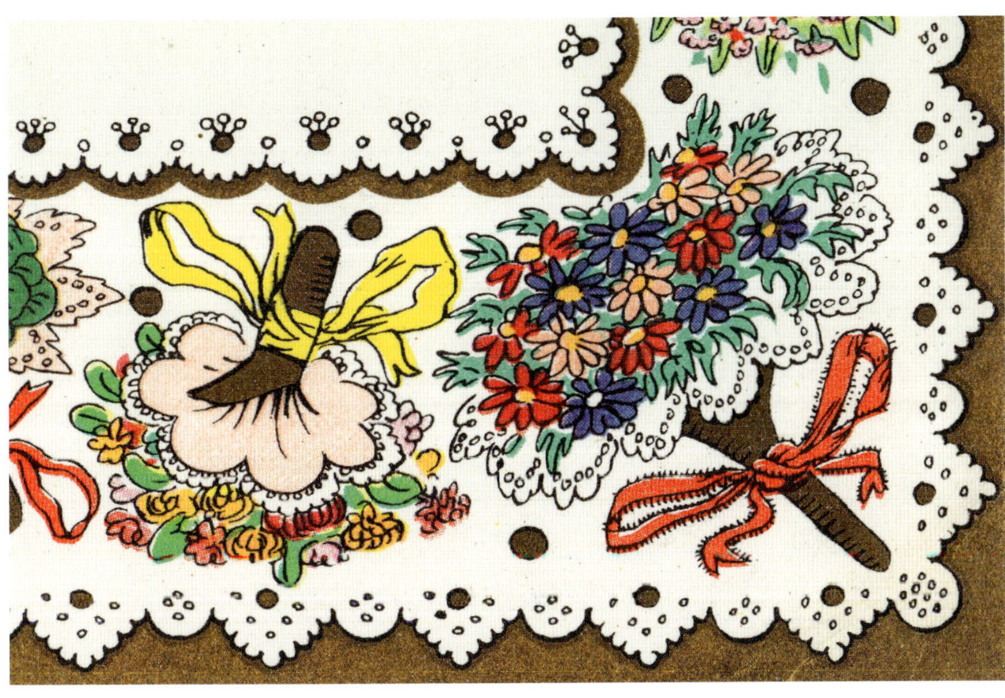

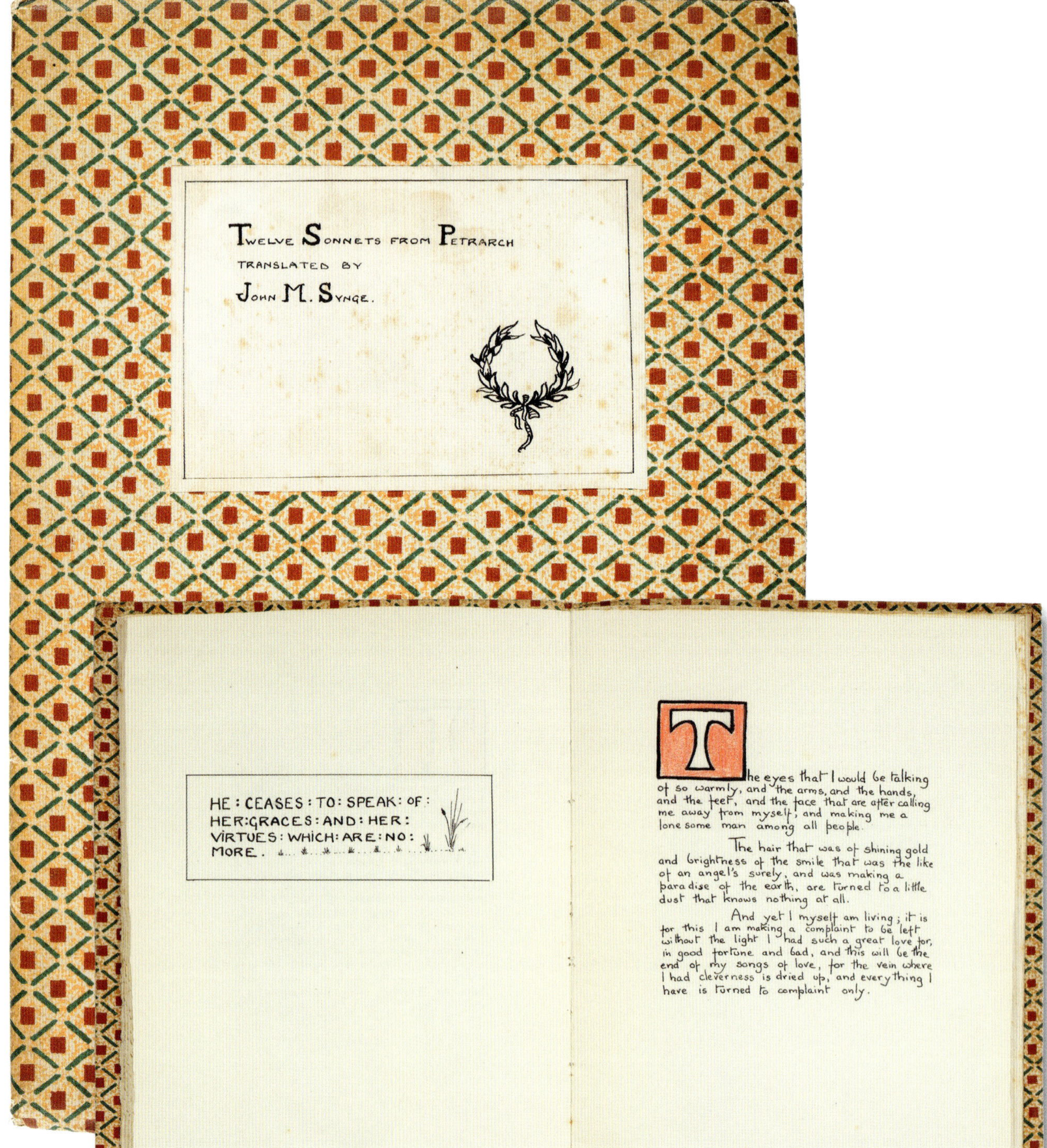
Twelve Sonnets from Petrarch
Translated by
John M. Synge.

HE : CEASES : TO : SPEAK : OF :
HER : GRACES : AND : HER :
VIRTUES : WHICH : ARE : NO :
MORE .

The eyes that I would be talking of so warmly, and the arms, and the hands, and the feet, and the face that are after calling me away from myself, and making me a lonesome man among all people.

The hair that was of shining gold and brightness of the smile that was the like of an angel's surely, and was making a paradise of the earth, are turned to a little dust that knows nothing at all.

And yet I myself am living; it is for this I am making a complaint to be left without the light I had such a great love for, in good fortune and bad, and this will be the end of my songs of love, for the vein where I had cleverness is dried up, and everything I have is turned to complaint only.

BOOK ILLUSTRATION

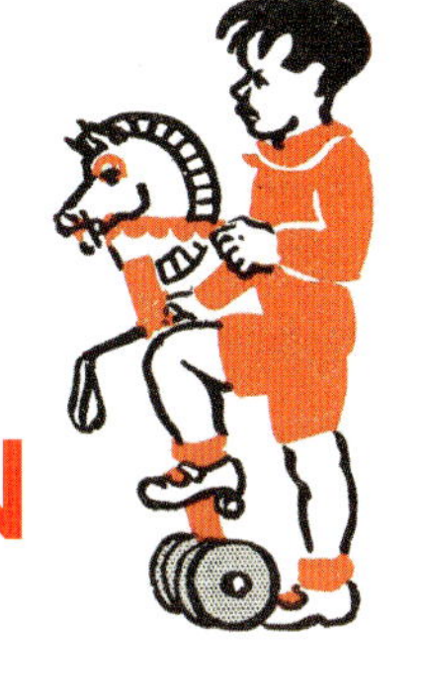

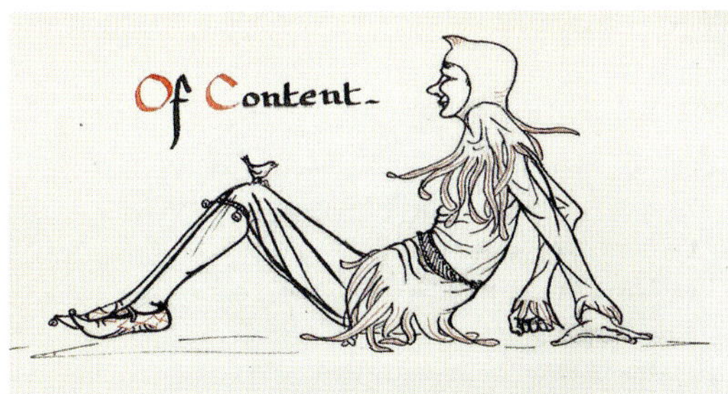

Above: *Seven Songs and One More* by William Dunbar, self-published 1924, 290 × 200 mm

Opposite: *Twelve Sonnets from Petrarch*, self-published 1924, 290 × 200 mm

One of the least known aspects of Herry's work is her book illustration. This was sometimes for her own books but more frequently for other authors.

She produced and illustrated *Twelve Sonnets from Petrarch* (translated by John M. Synge) in 1924. There is one handwritten copy only, dedicated to a Miss Mabel Rivers Currie. Miss Currie may have been a fellow student at the Central and, as she was married in December 1924, this could have been a wedding present. The book is fairly crudely done, with basic initials and decorations, but the patterned wrappers are good. Herry created a similar book for her godmother, Dorothy Palgrave Featherstone, for her birthday in 1924. Entitled *Seven Songs and One More*, it featured work by the Scottish poet William Dunbar (1459/60–c.1530), who reappeared on one of her best posters (see the 'Maps and Posters' section). The year 1924 was early days for her at the Central, and she would go on to pick up more skills from her teachers there. There are two other manuscripts by Herry from this period: one of Psalm 45, another of Proverbs 30.

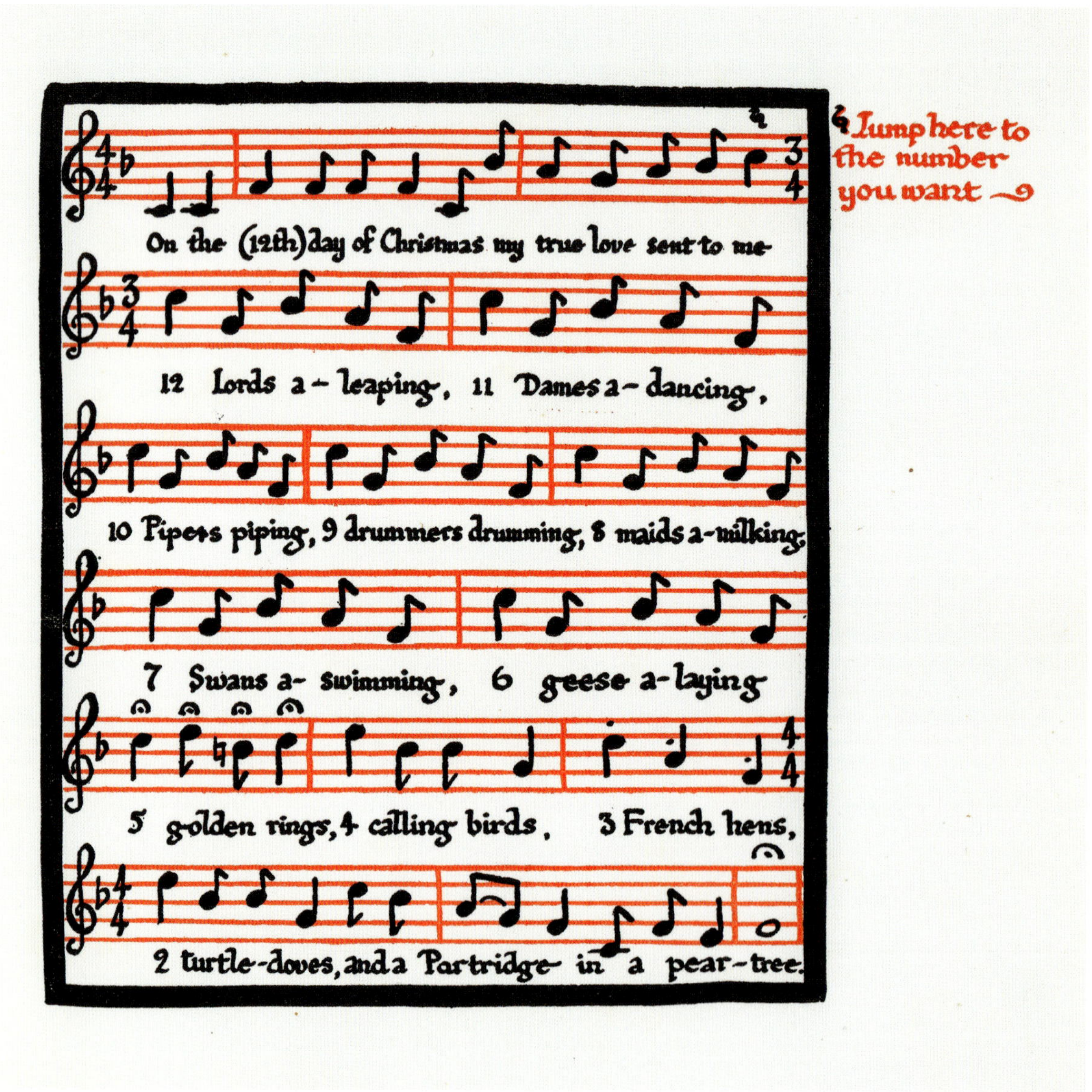

The Twelve Presents, created by Herry and published by Basil Blackwell in 1926, recounted the twelve days of Christmas according to the old Christmas song. It was dedicated to the politician Sir Raymond Greene, 2nd Baronet (1869–1947), but there is no information as to why. This was an attractive and much more assured production than those detailed above, with beautiful lettering and amusing drawings.

Above and opposite: *The Twelve Presents,* Basil Blackwell, Oxford, 1926, 253 x 190 mm

ON THE 4th DAY OF CHRISTMAS

My true-love sent to me—
Four calling birds,
Three French hens,
Two turtle-doves
And a partridge in a pear-tree—

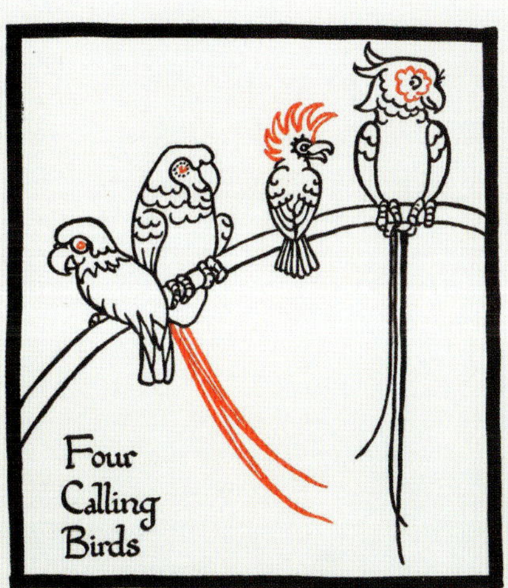

ON THE 12th DAY OF CHRISTMAS

My true-love sent to me—
Twelve lords a-leaping,
Eleven dames a-dancing,
Ten pipers piping,
Nine drummers drumming,
Eight maids a-milking,
Seven swans a-swimming,
Six geese a-laying,
Five golden rings,
Four calling birds,
Three French hens,
Two turtle-doves
And a partridge in a pear-tree.

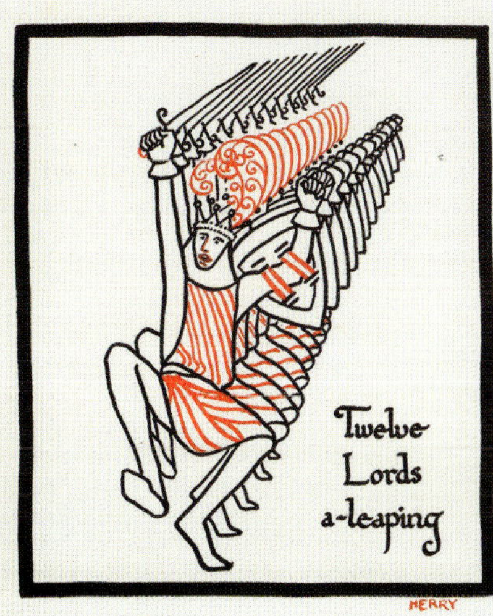

Next, she collaborated in 1930 on a book by
Hubert Steel called *Lighter London*, a humorous
look in verse at London streets, published by
G. Delgado. Herry-Perry (as she called herself
for this book) contributed amusing drawings.
They also worked together on a Stock
Exchange Calendar for 1931 (see page 34).

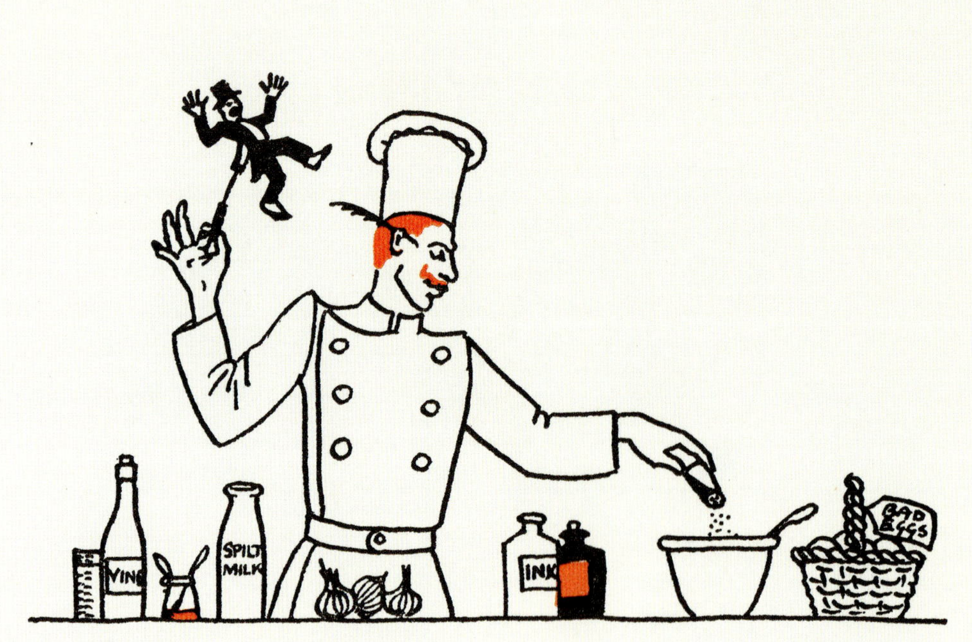

FLEET STREET

We frequent the Cheshire Cheese.
(Fleet Street, as you know, of course)
Once the Chef, who strives to please,
Told us of his latest sauce.

Above and opposite: pages from *Lighter London,*
verses by Hubert Steel, G. Delgado, London,
1930, 280 x 220 mm

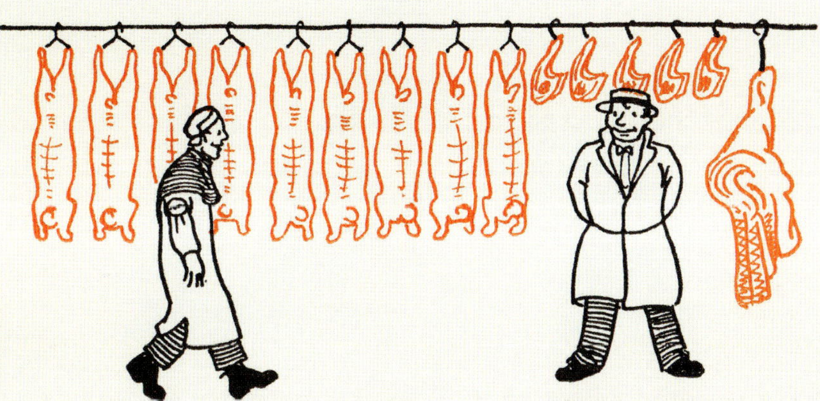

SMITHFIELD MARKET

Deferring to the artist's mild request,
I pen of Smithfield Market here a jest.
To find a theme, I trod with wearying feet
That Pantheon of finest home-killed meat.
Here the prime beef attains its apogee,
Here swings the sheep, from woolly covering free.
Hygiene's high priest—let every drunkard shiver
Decrees the end of any evil liver.
"Enough"—you cry? I grant you then relief—
There's little humour in a side of beef.

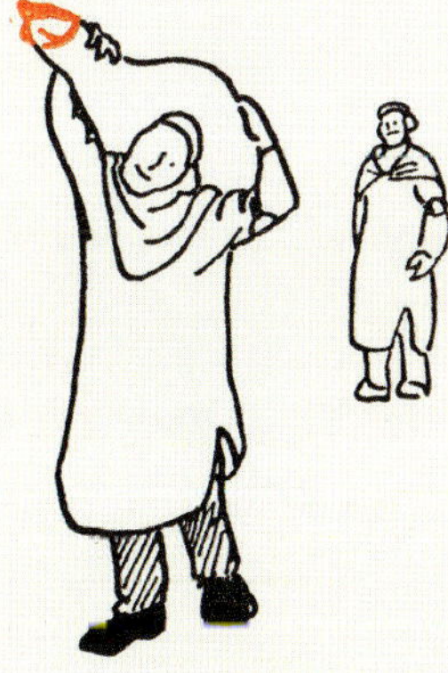

BILLINGSGATE 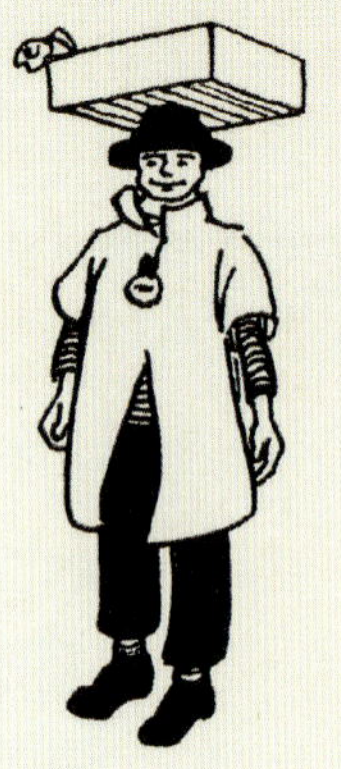 FISHMARKET

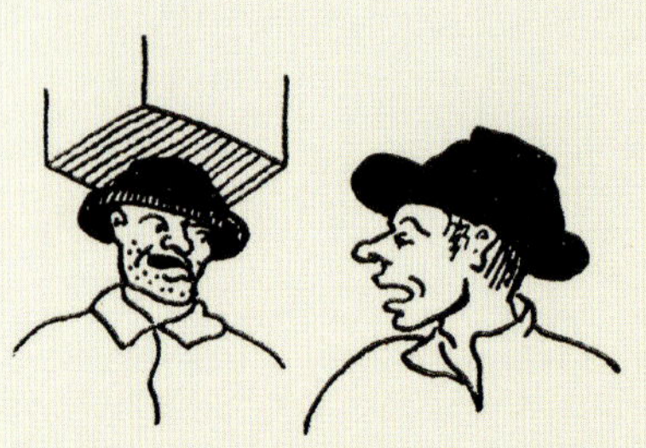

I went down to Billingsgate Market:
The language is awful, they say.

But all I could hear was "Good-morning, ol'dear,"
And "Kindly step out of my way."
Not one of the porters said "Bother,"
Not once did I have to blush red,
But a porter named Joe put his boot on my toe,
And *I* used some language instead.

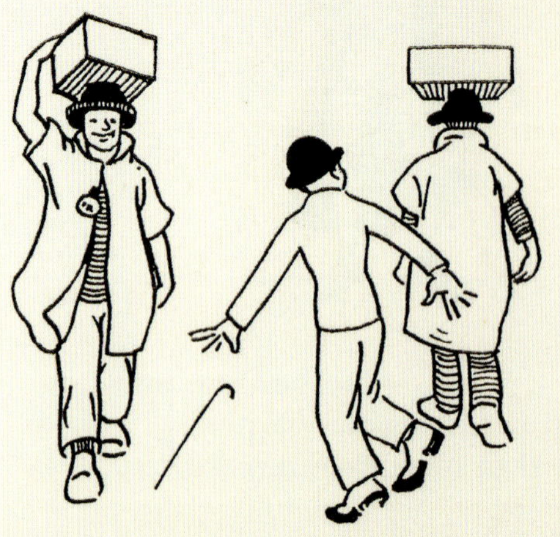

43

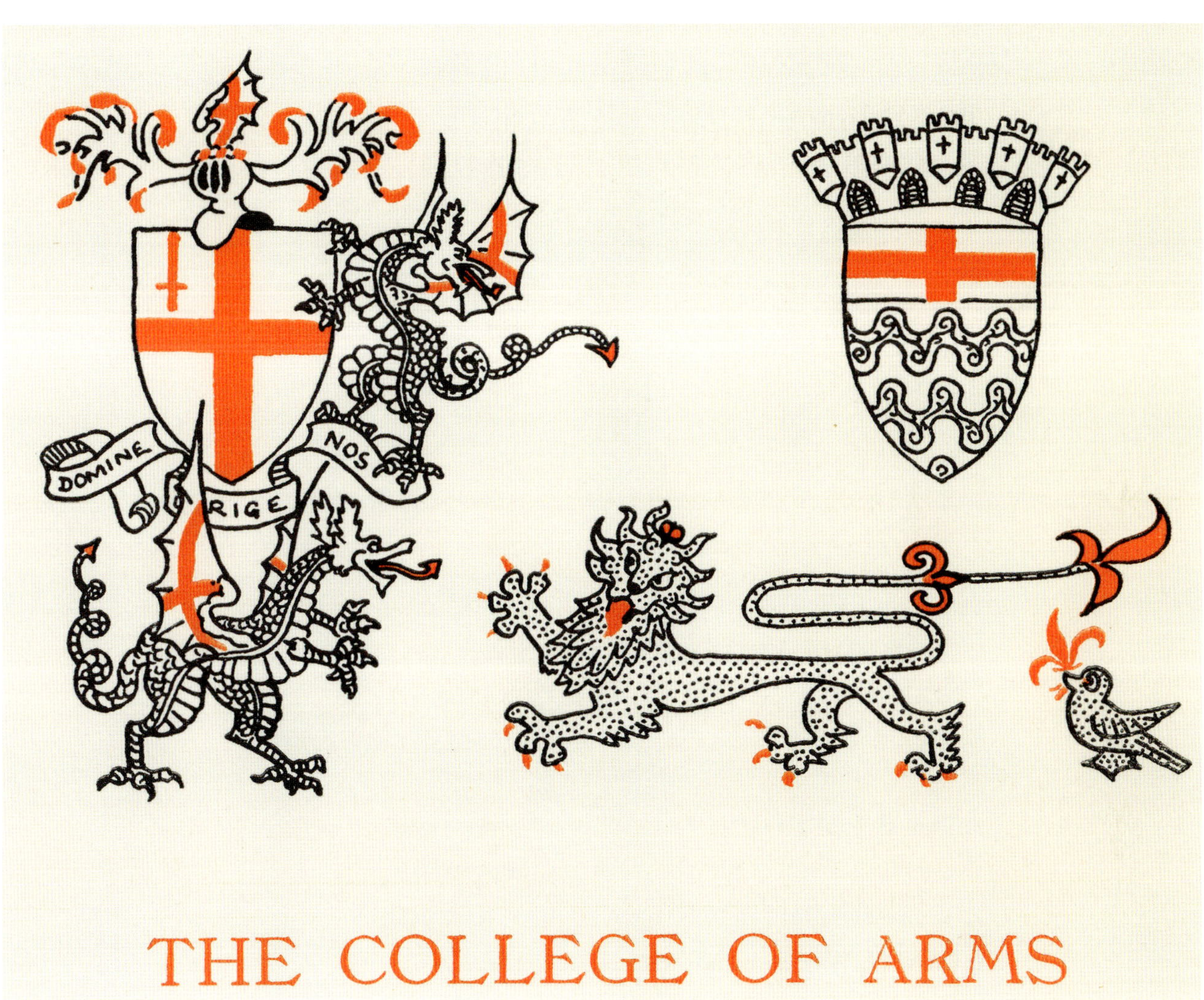

Above and opposite: pages and details from
Lighter London, verses by Hubert Steel,
G. Delgado, London, 1930, 280 x 220 mm

Opposite inset: dedication from *Lighter London*

THE COLLEGE OF ARMS

The Dragons and the Leopard (passant gardant)
Engaged in heated argument one morn.
Their angry passions rose to fever ardent,
And nearly spoiled the scutcheons they adorn.

A martlet, or, who on a field improper
Was nibbling at a fleur-de-lys, in gules,
Was so annoyed he went and fetched a copper,
Which is, of course, against heraldic rules.

When charged before a King-at-Arms, each creature
Revealed himself as quite a legal twister.
The case presented many a curious feature—
They got two years behind a bar sinister.

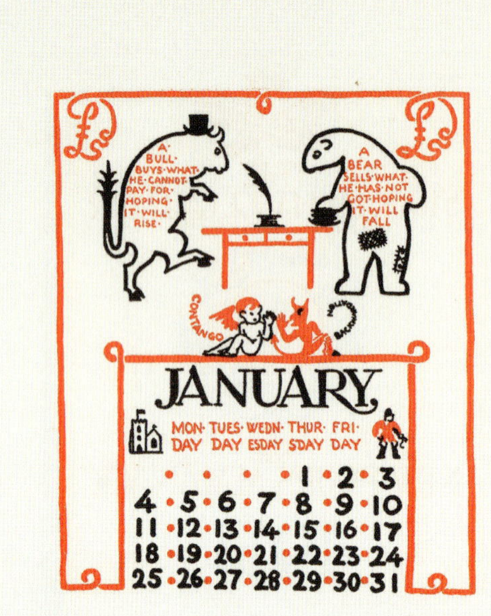

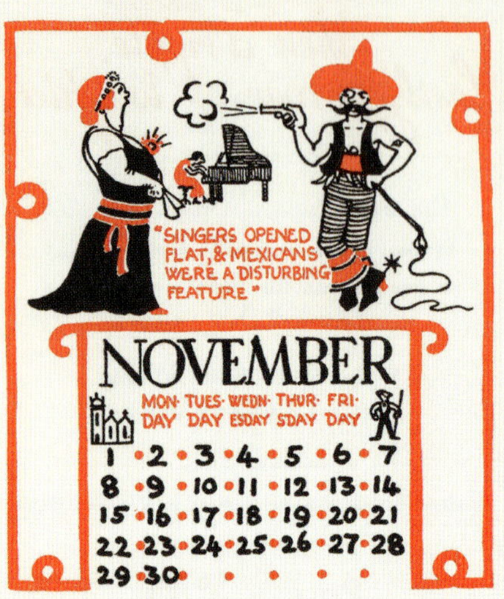

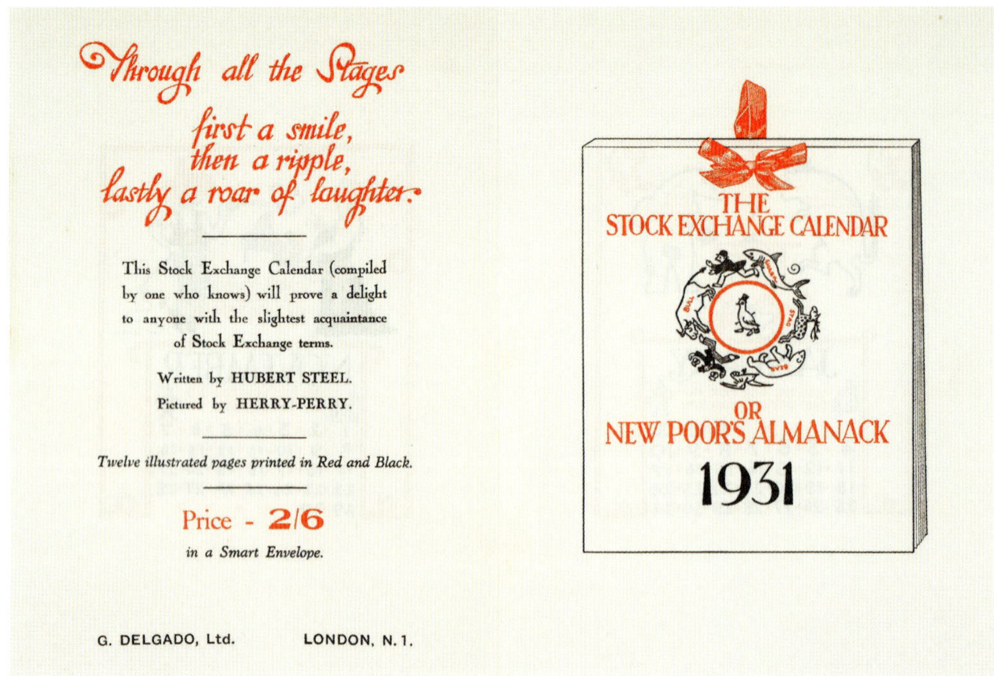

Above: Flyer for *The Stock Exchange Calendar or New Poor's Almanack*, G. Delgado, London, 1930, 175 x 120 mm

In 1933, Herry illustrated *Animals Limited*, a children's book by James Cook (published by Artists and Writers Guild, Inc.). As is clear from images shown elsewhere in this book, Herry was very good at bringing animals to life and making them amusing. She also collaborated, in 1936, with writer Kathleen Wallace on another children's book called *The House with the Key*, but I have not been able to find a copy of it.

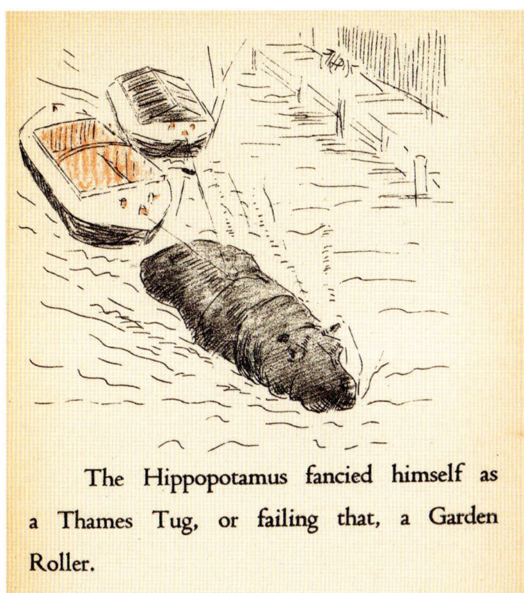

The Hippopotamus fancied himself as a Thames Tug, or failing that, a Garden Roller.

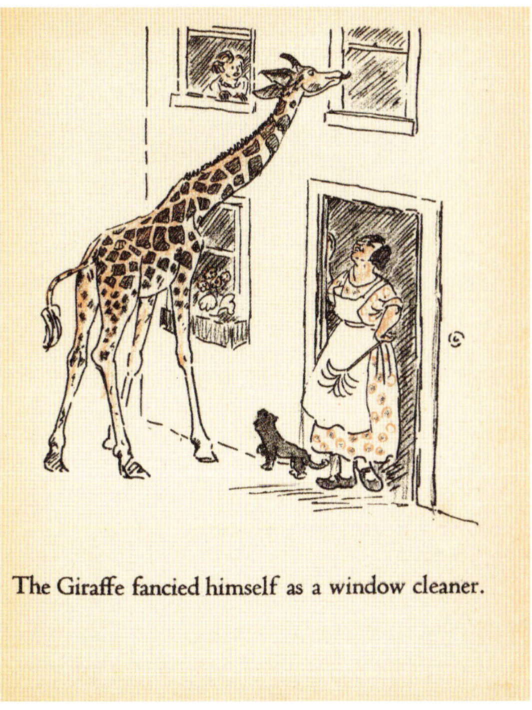

The Giraffe fancied himself as a window cleaner.

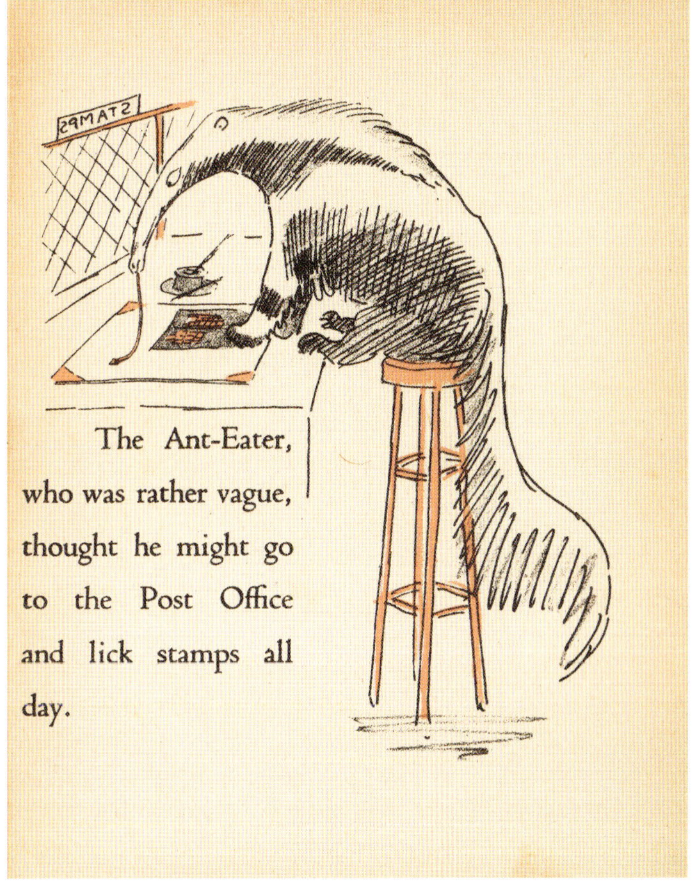

The Ant-Eater, who was rather vague, thought he might go to the Post Office and lick stamps all day.

Above: *Animals Limited* by James Cook, Artists and Writers Guild Inc., Poughkeepsie, New York, 1933, 221 x 162 mm

In the same year that she worked on *Animals Limited*, 1933, Herry turned to very different subject-matter by illustrating food writer Elizabeth Craig's *Entertaining with Elizabeth Craig*, published by Collins. This was an all-encompassing manual for the young housewife on how to become an ideal hostess and included many recipes. Herry's colourful drawings enhance the recipes and the etiquette lessons.

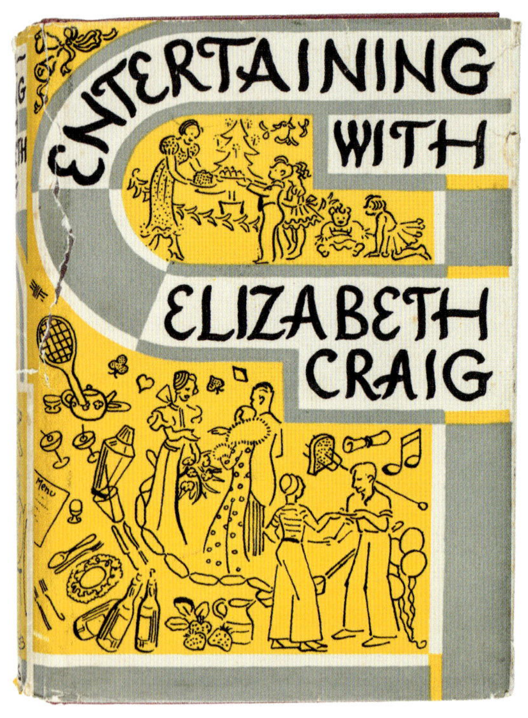

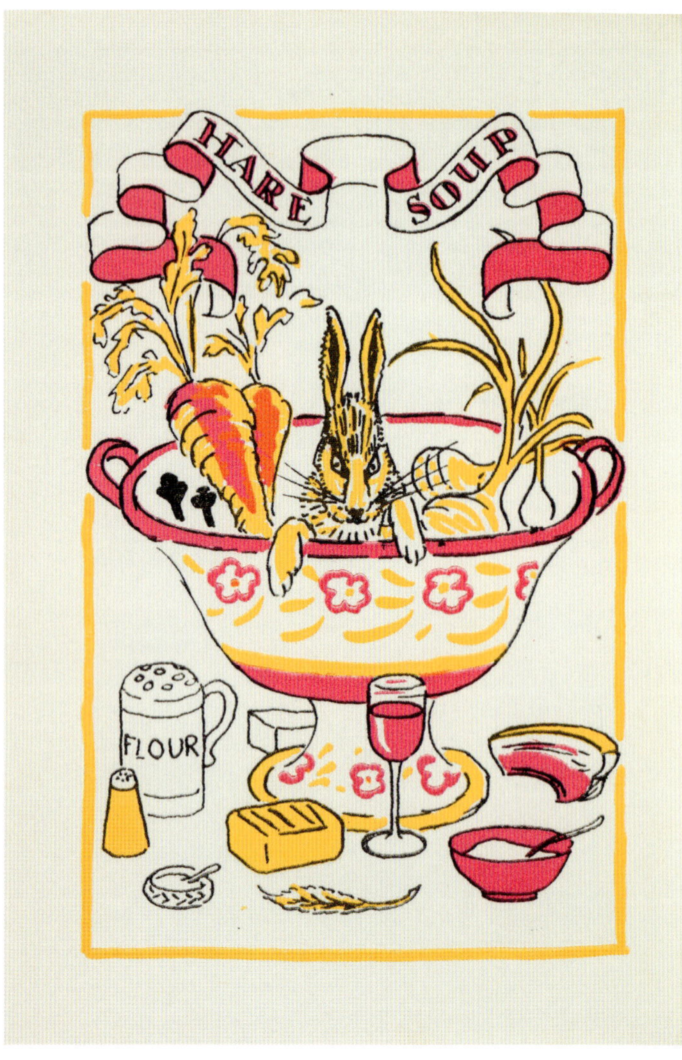

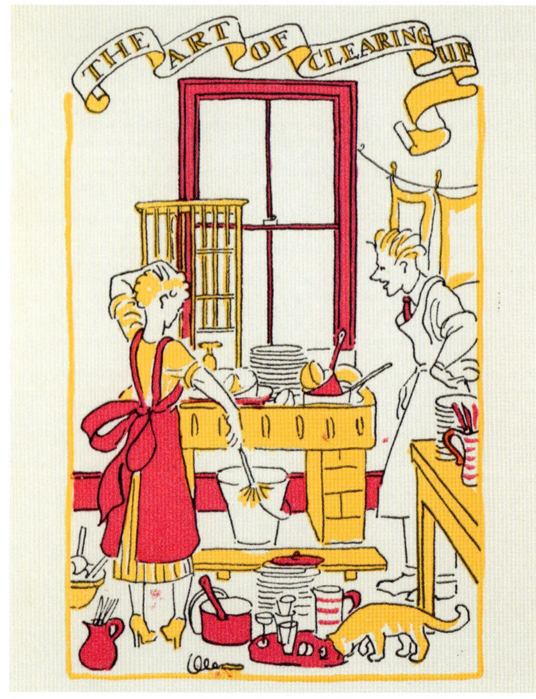

Above and opposite: Cover and pages from *Entertaining with Elizabeth Craig* by Elizabeth Craig, Collins, London, 1933, 187 x 120 mm

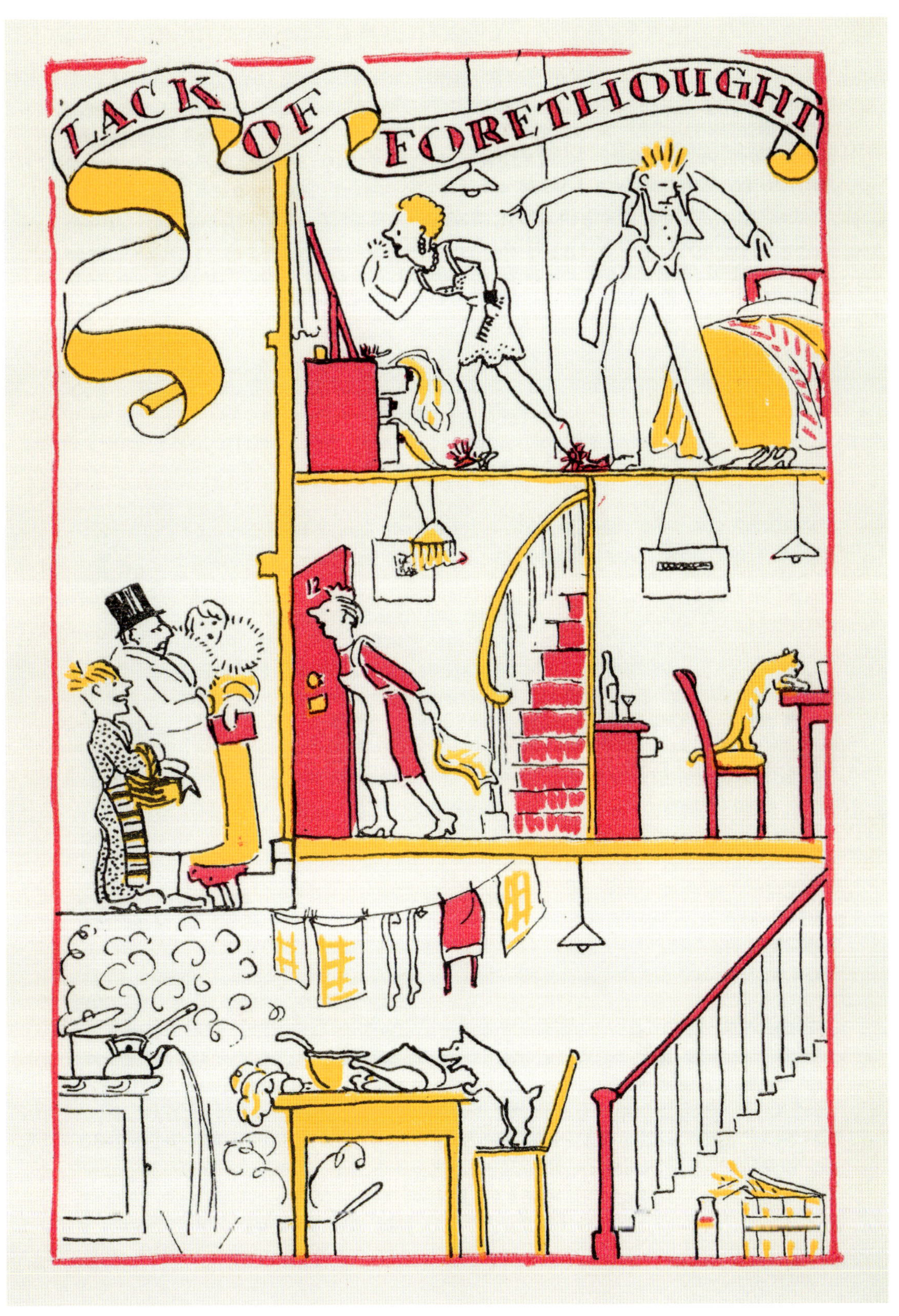

LACK OF FORETHOUGHT

Turning again to children's books, but of a different kind, between 1939 and 1942 Herry illustrated a number of *Beacon* arithmetic books (published by Ginn & Company) that were reprinted repeatedly until at least 1959. She succeeded in making the books less dry than they might have been, by using numerous lively illustrations.

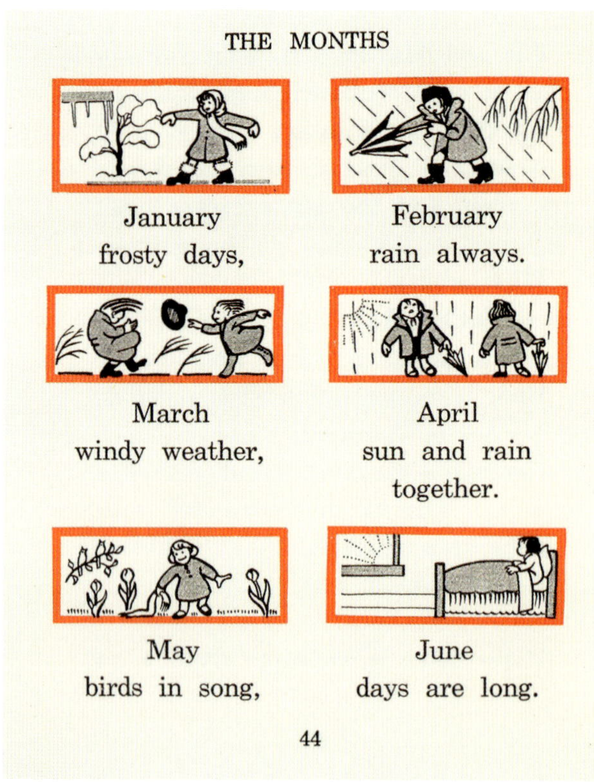

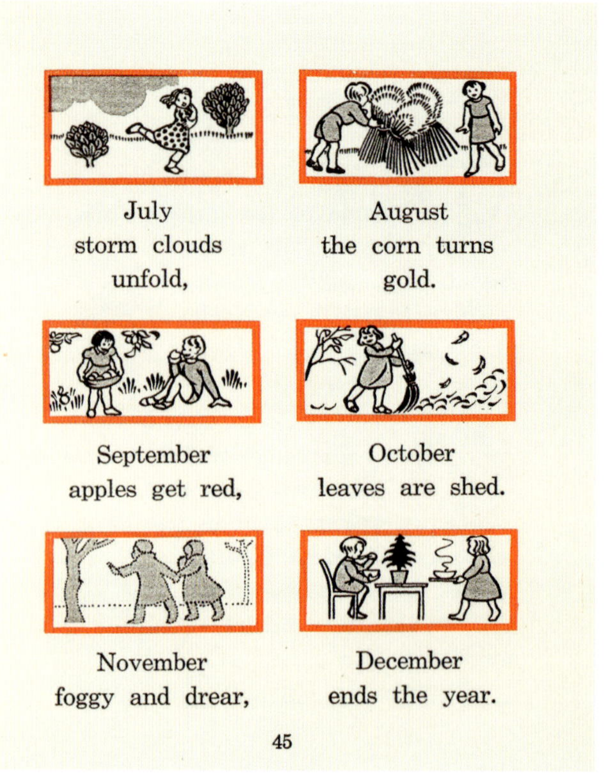

Above left and right: *Beacon Number Reader* by C.M. Fleming and E. Grassam, Ginn and Company, London, 1939, 208 x 152 mm

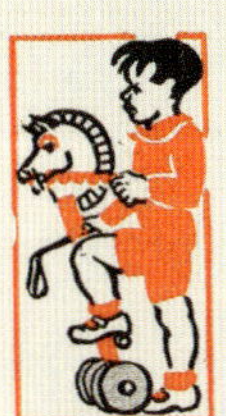

RIDE - A - COCK - HORSE

Ride - a - cock - horse,
To Banbury Cross,
To see what Tommy can buy.
A penny white loaf,
A penny white cake,
And a twopenny apple pie.

How many things altogether can Tommy buy at Banbury Cross?

What is the difference between the cost of a white loaf and an apple pie?

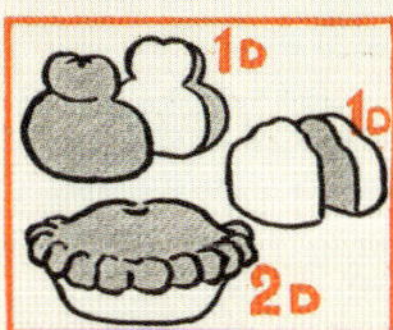
Here are a loaf, a cake and an apple pie. Which have been cut into two equal parts? Draw the things which have been cut into halves?

74

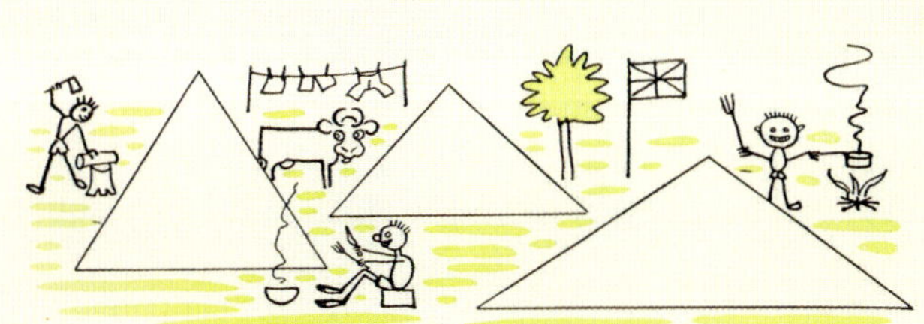

These are tents which Tom drew after Jim had been to the camp. Copy them in your book.
This is a new kind of shape.

1. How many corners has each shape?
2. Measure the corners with your " right angle ".
        Are there any right angles?
Shapes like these with three corners or *angles* are called *triangles*.
3. Do you know how to make a paper bag for sweets or a paper hat like these :

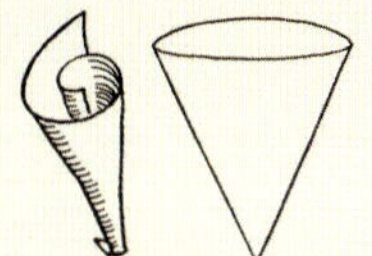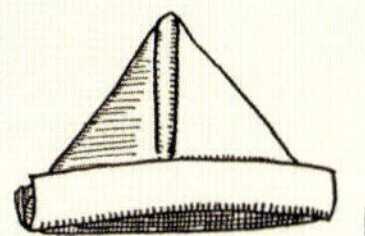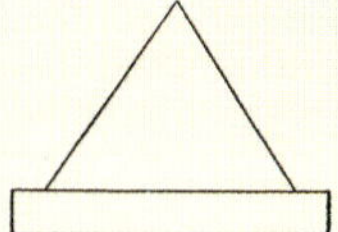

Get some paper and make a hat and a bag.
46

Above left and right: *Beacon Arithmetic, Book Two Part Two* by C.M. Fleming, Ginn and Company, London, 1939, 208 x 152 mm

In 1940, using her experience as a Voluntary Aid Detachment nurse, Herry wrote a book with a doctor, David York, entitled *First Aid for First-Aiders or 'What'll I Do?'* (published by Hutchinson & Co.). This was meant to enlighten and entertain people about basic first aid in a humorous way, although some people may not find the humour so funny these days.

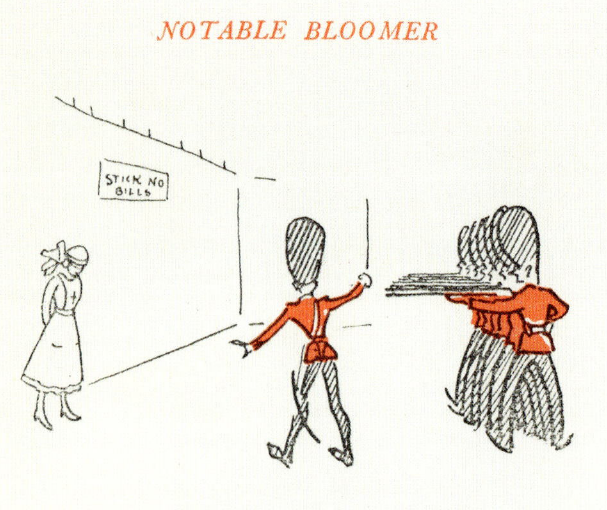

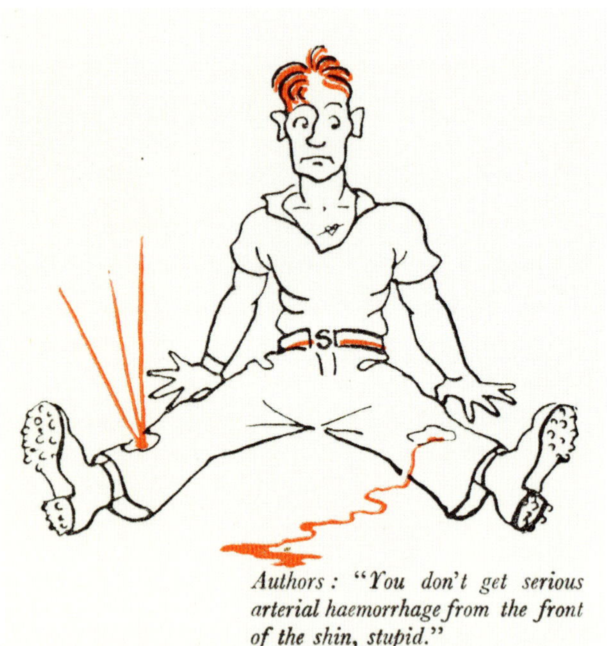

Top: Dedication from *First Aid for First-Aiders or 'What'll I Do?'* by Herry-Perry and David York, Hutchinson & Co., London, 1940, 185 x 120 mm

Left and above: Pages from *First Aid for First-Aiders or 'What'll I Do?'*

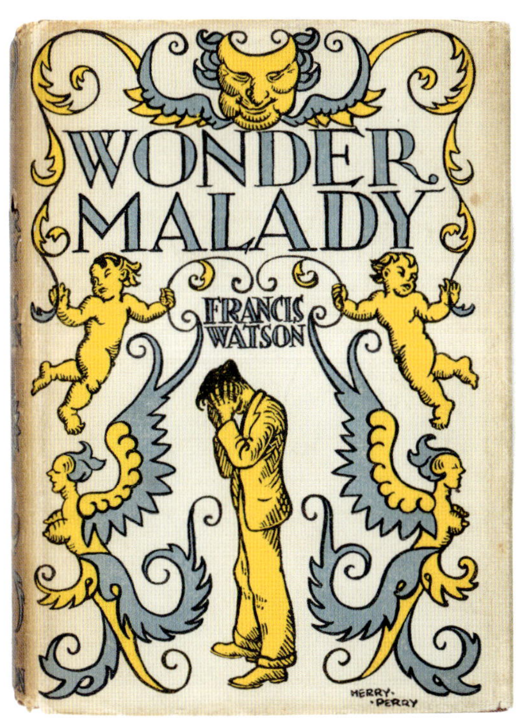

Herry also designed two book dust-jackets. One was for *Wonder Malady* by Francis Watson (Lovat Dickson, 1933) and the other for *The Man in Our Lives* by John Guthrie (Thomas Nelson & Sons, 1946), both of which have deservedly sunk without trace!

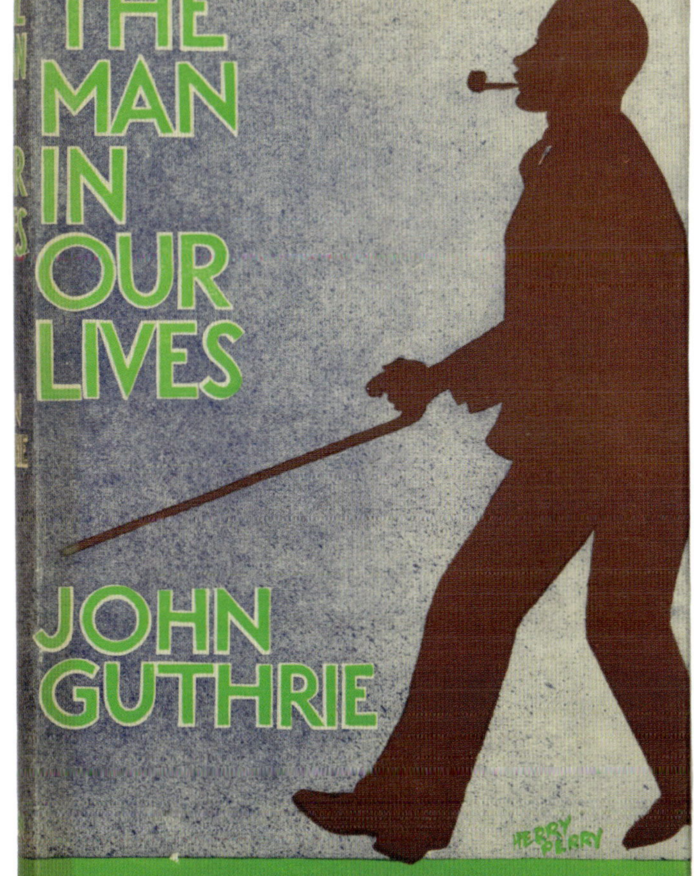

Above: Book jacket for *Wonder Malady* by Francis Watson, Lovat Dickson, London, 1933, 183 x 120 mm

Right: Book jacket for *The Man In Our Lives* by John Guthrie, Thomas Nelson & Sons, 1946, 205 x 140 mm

LAWRENCE'S RIDES
October 1917
January 1918
The Yarmuk Raid : The Mining at Minifer :
The Spying in the Hauran : The Battle at Tafileh :
MILES
100
Mediterranean Sea
Damascus
HAURAN
Haifa
Sheik Saad
Tafas
Gadara
Tel Shehab
Arar
Mezerib
Deraa
JEBEL
Remthe
DRUSE
Nisib
Minifer
Abu Sawana
Amman
Azrak
Jericho
Hesban
Jerusalem
Dead Sea
Amari
Gaza
Sirhan
El Arish
Beersheba
Kerak
Desert
SINAI
Tafileh
Bair
Petra
Maan
Jefer
Delagha
Waheida
Aba el
Lissan
Batra
Shediia
Guweira
Akaba
Rumm
Red Sea
HERRY PERRY

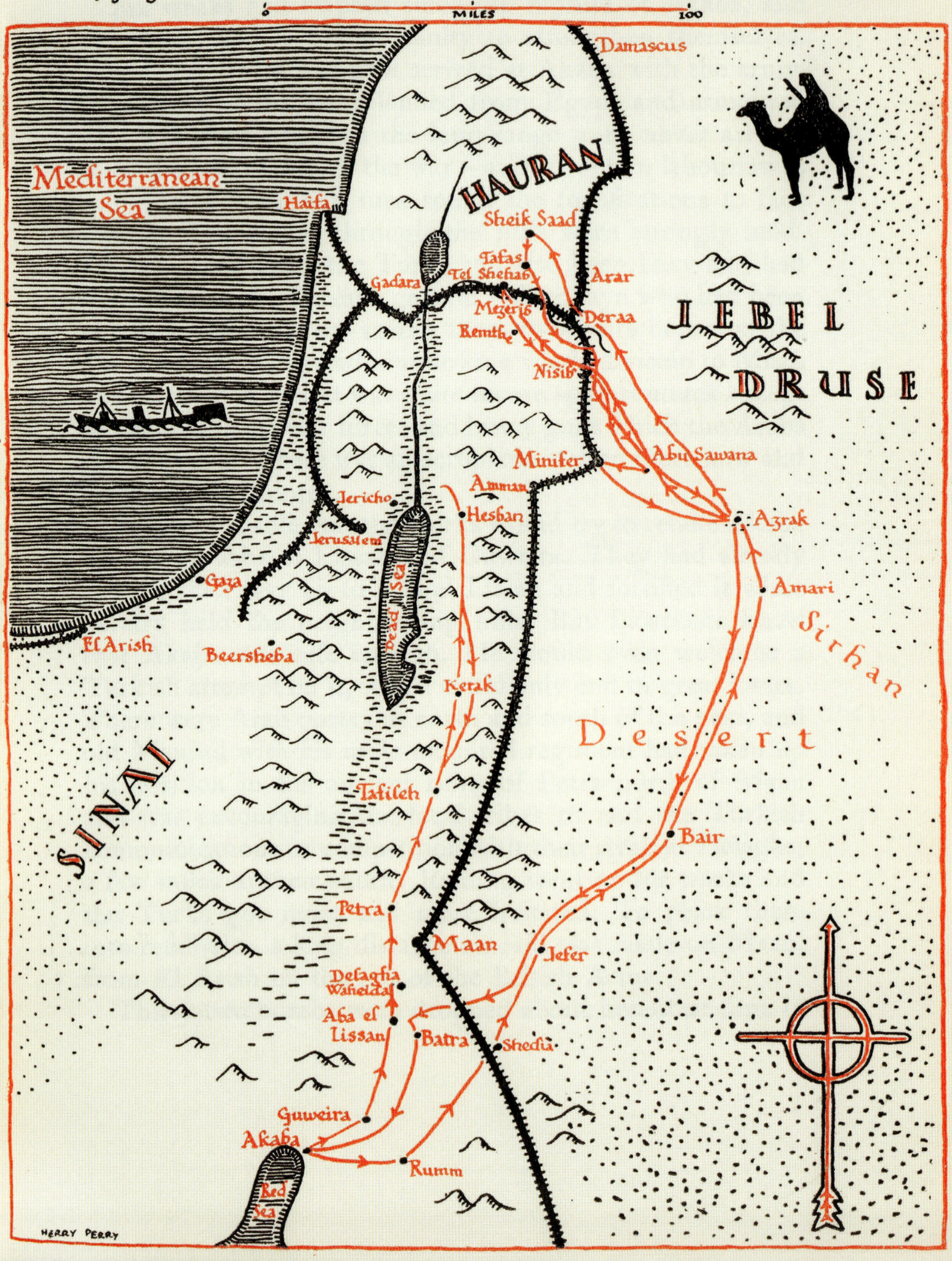

MAPS and POSTERS

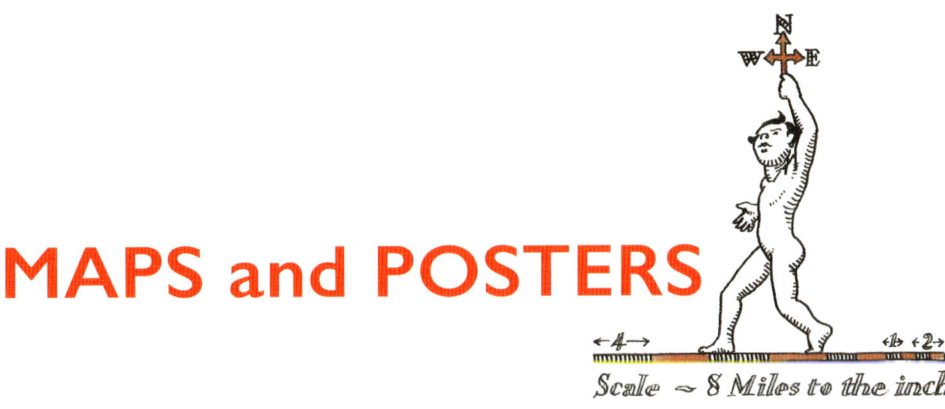

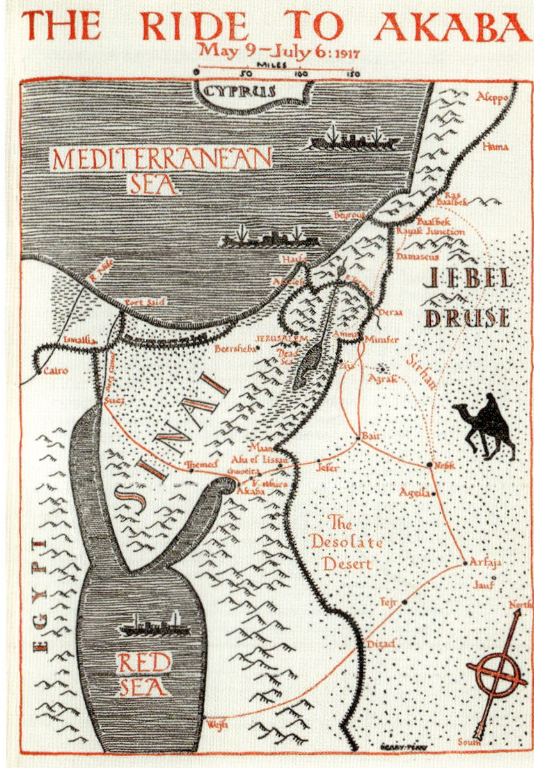

Above and opposite: Maps from *Lawrence and the Arabs* by Robert Graves, Jonathan Cape, London, 1927, 200 x 140 mm

The curriculum at the Central School of Arts and Crafts was very broad, with an emphasis on crafts. This can be seen from Herry's wood engraving of the Central (see page 6), which shows all the various teaching departments. It is therefore no surprise that Herry produced a wide range of art and crafts in various media. One of her most prolific areas was posters and maps (maps in books, maps as murals and maps in posters). This book's 'Murals' section deals with the map murals at Rothamsted Experimental Station and on R.M.S. *Queen Mary*, although there were others which we no longer have images of (for example that done for Sir Julien Cahn, 1st Baronet).

In 1927, in her last year at the Central, she was commissioned by publishers Jonathan Cape to produce three maps for Robert Graves's book *Lawrence and the Arabs*, a biography of Lawrence of Arabia (T.E. Lawrence). It's not clear how this commission came about but it marked her out as someone who could produce accurate and attractive maps.

It was 1927 that also marked the beginning of her association with London Transport (in its various guises) and its chief executive Frank Pick (1878–1941). (See page 88 for a list of Herry's posters for London Transport and other clients.) Frank Pick was instrumental in developing and modernising London Transport's advertising campaigns as London Underground expanded into the city's suburbs and he sought to increase the use of buses, trams, underground and overground trains and coaches across the network. Herry's first two posters (*The Empire Under One Roof* and *A New Chart of the Royal Zoological Society's Gardens in Regent's Park*) perhaps look a little old-fashioned compared to other artists' London Transport posters at that time, and to Herry's later posters, but they get their message across clearly and are designed well. They both include intricate maps and *The Empire under One Roof* includes heraldry – features that will recur in later artwork.

In 1928, she did another poster of London Zoo, *The Zoo Alphabet*, comprising an inventive A–Z of animals. And *Derby Day* marked the start of a more modern style for her, with bold colours and plenty of movement. It also shows her witty side, as it is based on Paolo Uccello's painting *The Battle of San Romano* (c.1439). The same year, 1928, saw Herry exhibiting for the first time at the annual exhibition of the Arts and Crafts Exhibition Society, which had been founded in 1887 to promote the decorative arts. Her inclusion was to be expected as the society's exhibitions covered the crafts

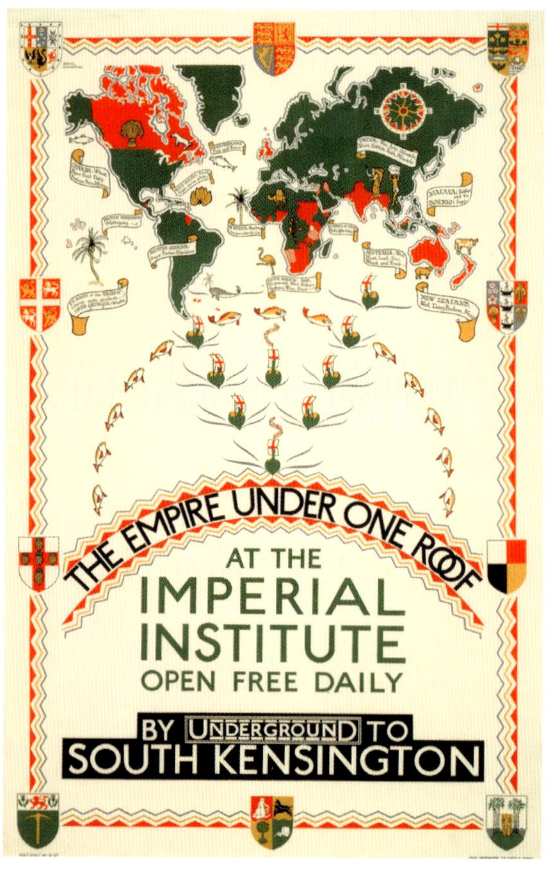

Above: *The Empire Under One Roof,* Double Royal poster, 1927, 1016 x 635 mm (© TfL from the London Transport Museum collection)

Opposite: *A New Chart of the Royal Zoological Society's Gardens in Regent's Park*, Double Royal poster, 1927, 1016 x 635 mm (© TfL from the London Transport Museum collection)

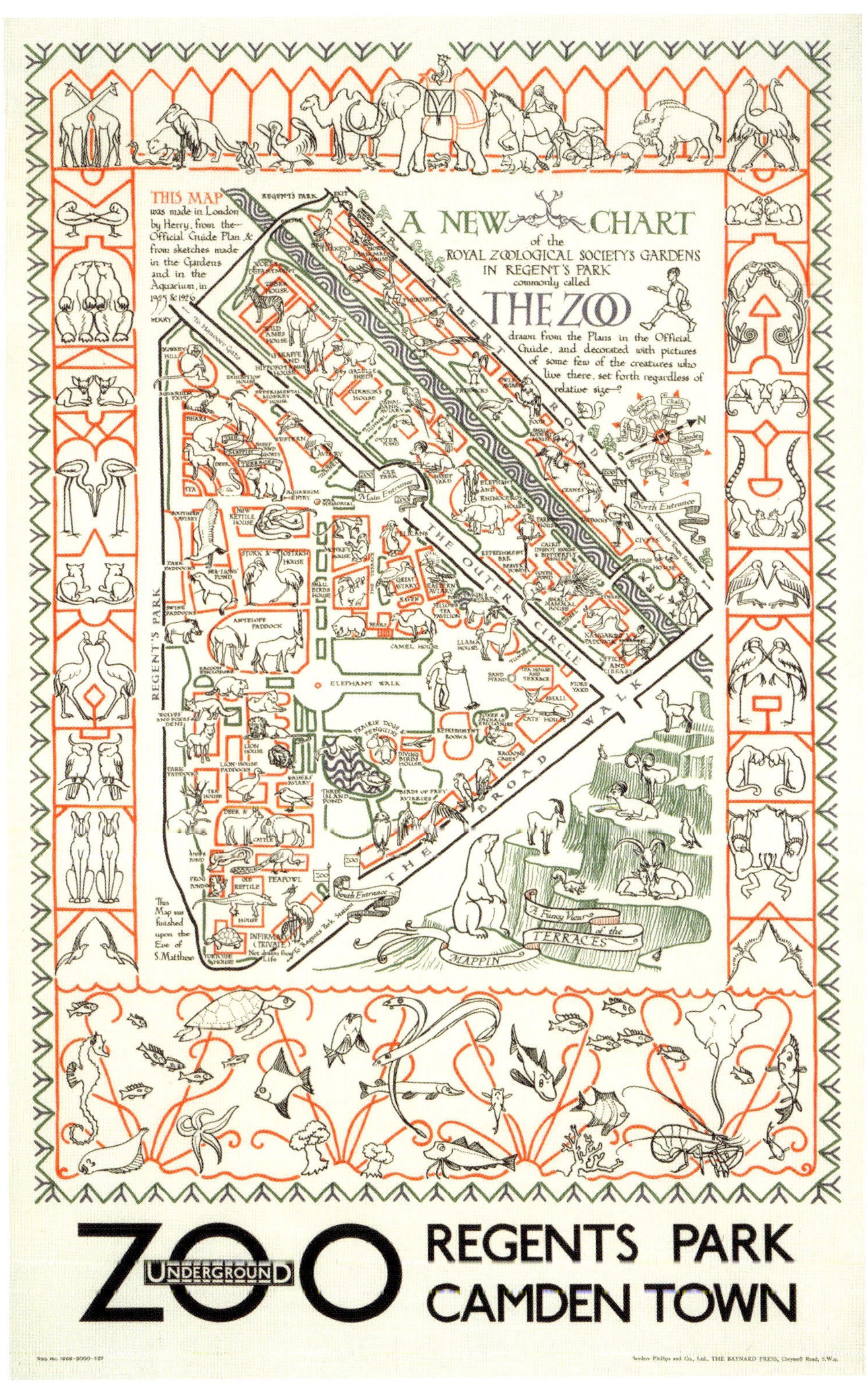

ZOO REGENTS PARK CAMDEN TOWN

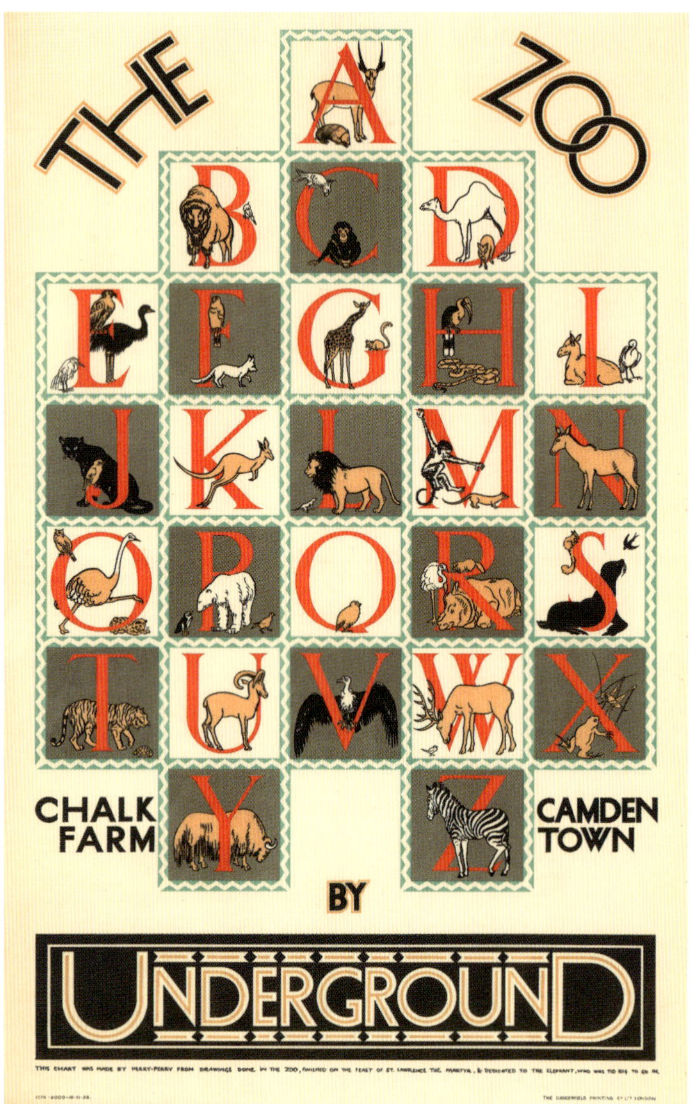

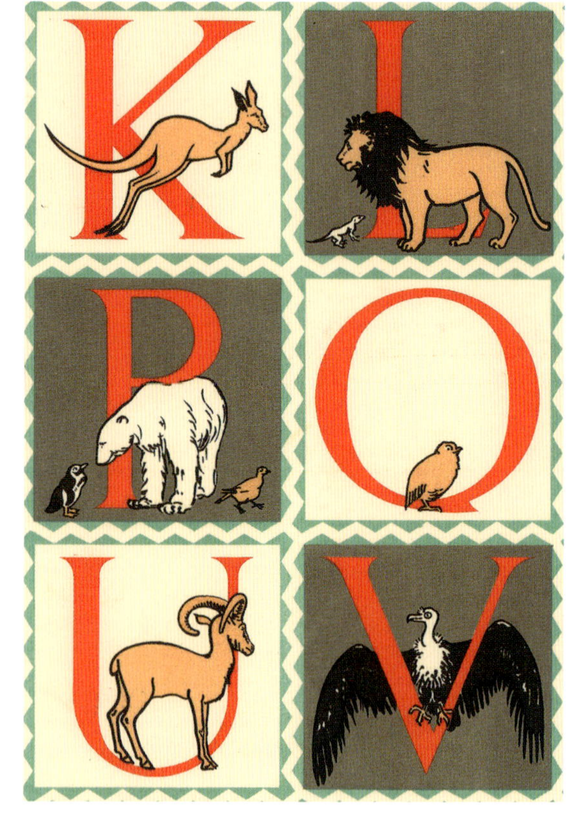

which Herry would have been taught at the Central. Noel Rooke (one of her teachers at the Central) and Joyce Clissold (one of her fellow students) were later on the council of the society, although it seems that Herry was never a member or lay member. She exhibited two items which, unfortunately, are poorly described: a house map on vellum and another house map (items 5 and 215 respectively in the exhibition catalogue).

Above left: *The Zoo Alphabet*, Double Royal poster, 1928, 1016 x 635 mm (© TfL from the London Transport Museum collection)

Above: Detail from *The Zoo Alphabet*

Opposite: *Derby Day,* poster, 1928, 292 x 469 mm (© TfL from the London Transport Museum collection)

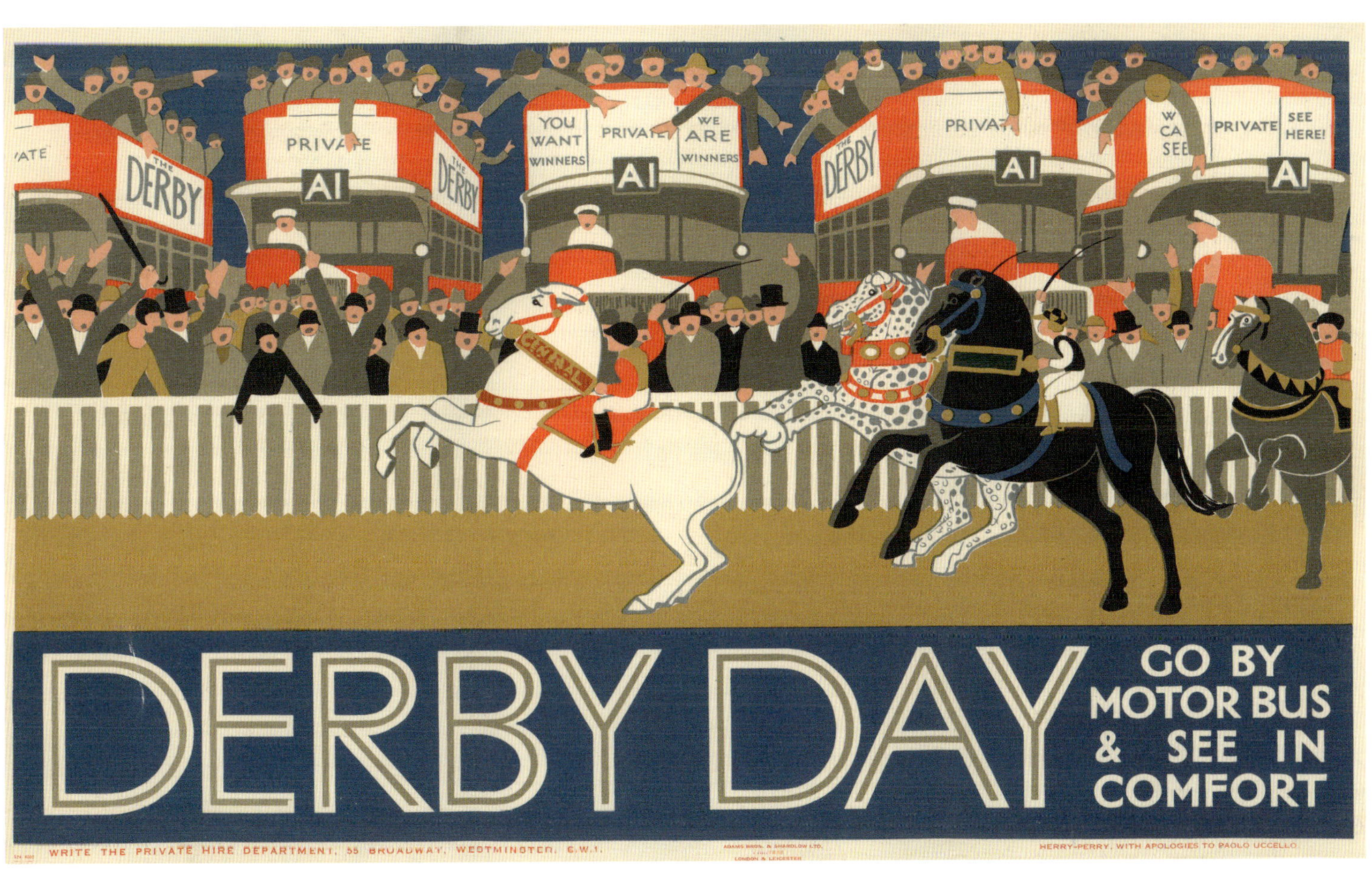
PRIVATE
THE DERBY
AI
YOU WANT WINNERS
PRIVATE
AI
WE ARE WINNERS
THE DERBY
PRIVATE
AI
W CA SEE
PRIVATE
SEE HERE!
AI
CENTRAL
DERBY DAY
GO BY MOTOR BUS & SEE IN COMFORT
WRITE THE PRIVATE HIRE DEPARTMENT, 55 BROADWAY, WESTMINSTER, S.W.1.
ADAMS BROS. & SHARDLOW LTD. LONDON & LEICESTER
HERRY-PERRY, WITH APOLOGIES TO PAOLO UCCELLO

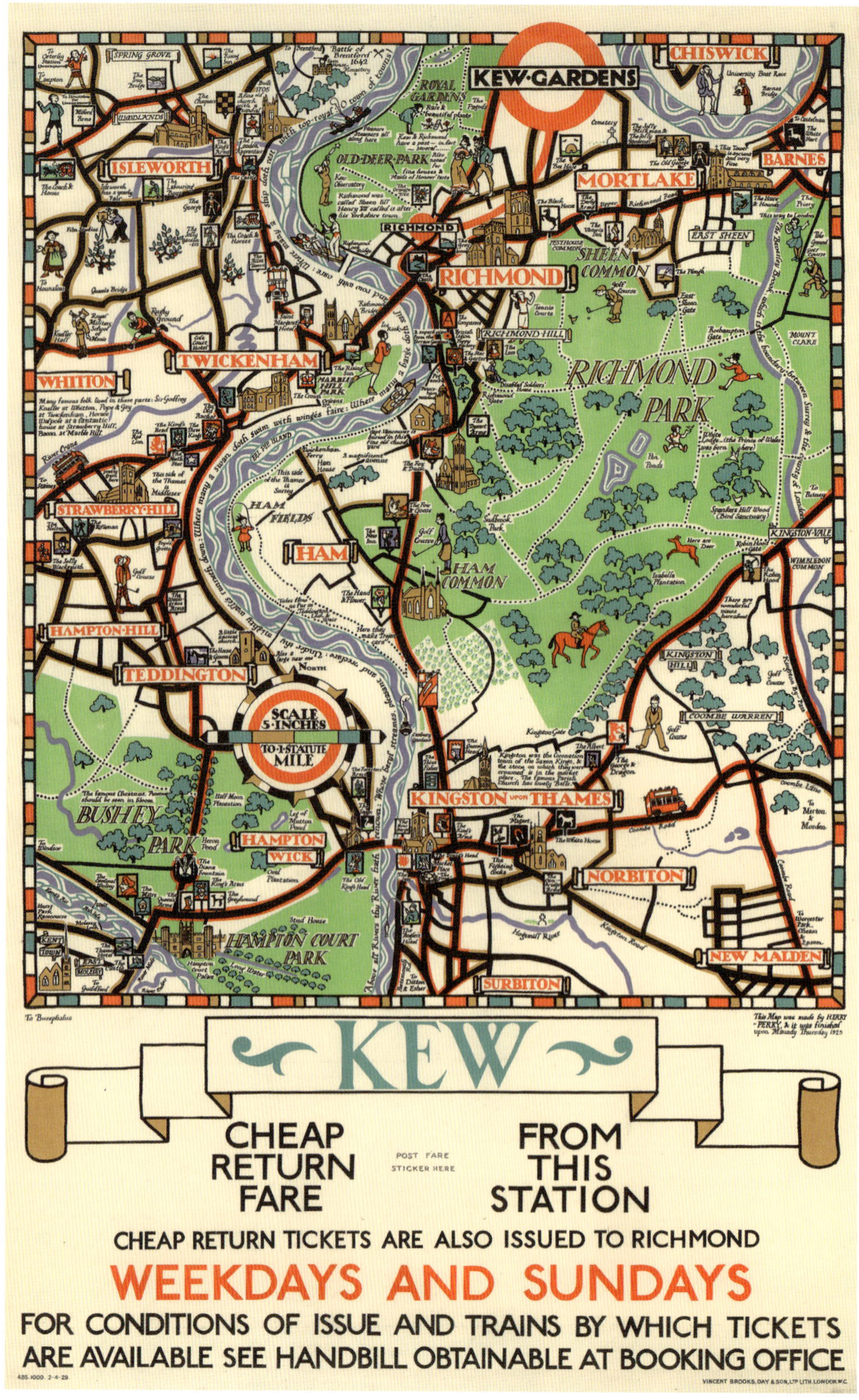

KEW·GARDENS
CHISWICK
ROYAL GARDENS
OLD·DEER·PARK
MORTLAKE
BARNES
ISLEWORTH
SPRING GROVE
RICHMOND
EAST SHEEN
SHEEN COMMON
TWICKENHAM
WHITTON
RICHMOND·HILL
RICHMOND PARK
MOUNT CLARE
STRAWBERRY·HILL
HAM FIELDS
HAM
HAM COMMON
KINGSTON·VALE
WIMBLEDON COMMON
HAMPTON·HILL
TEDDINGTON
SCALE 5·INCHES TO·1·STATUTE MILE
KINGSTON HILL
COOMBE WARREN
BUSHEY PARK
HAMPTON WICK
KINGSTON upon THAMES
NORBITON
HAMPTON COURT PARK
NEW MALDEN
SURBITON
KEW
This Map was made by HERRY PERRY, & it was finished upon Maundy Thursday 1925
CHEAP RETURN FARE
POST FARE STICKER HERE
FROM THIS STATION
CHEAP RETURN TICKETS ARE ALSO ISSUED TO RICHMOND
WEEKDAYS AND SUNDAYS
FOR CONDITIONS OF ISSUE AND TRAINS BY WHICH TICKETS
ARE AVAILABLE SEE HANDBILL OBTAINABLE AT BOOKING OFFICE
VINCENT BROOKS, DAY & SON, LTP LTH LONDON W.C.

The number of posters produced by Herry for London Transport increased in 1929. A series of five (all in the same style) were designed to encourage people to travel to the extremities of the Underground network and then walk in the countryside, rambling being a popular pastime then, or visit local towns and parks. One of the best of these is *Kew*, with its beautiful, detailed map showing attractions such as Kew Gardens and Bushey [Bushy] Park.

Opposite: *Kew*, Double Royal poster, 1929, 1016 x 635 mm (© TfL from the London Transport Museum collection)

Below: Details from *Kew*

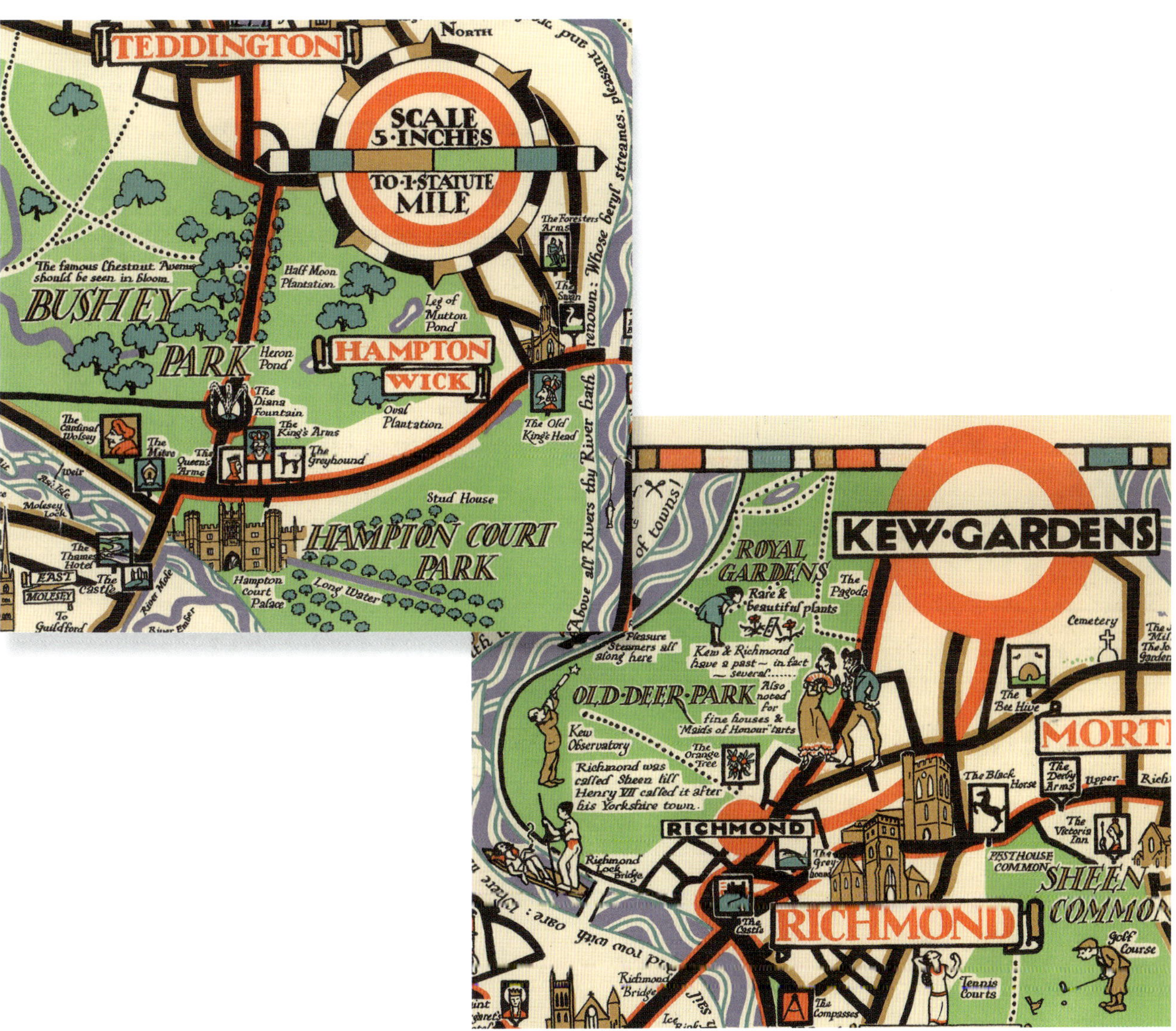

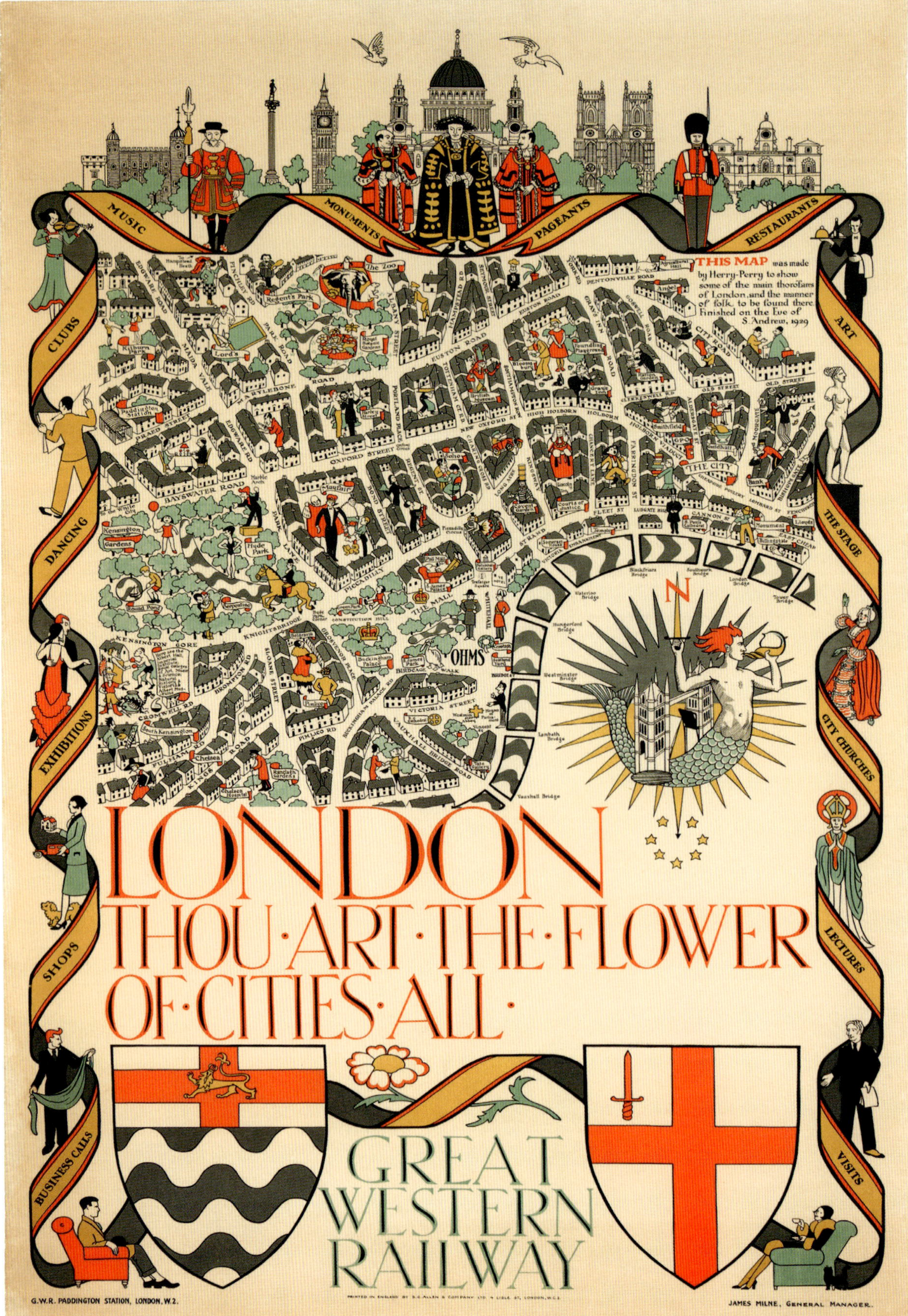
MUSIC
MONUMENTS
PAGEANTS
RESTAURANTS
CLUBS
ART
DANCING
THE STAGE
EXHIBITIONS
CITY CHURCHES
SHOPS
LECTURES
BUSINESS CALLS
VISITS
THIS MAP was made by Herry-Perry to show some of the main thorofares of London, and the manner of folk to be found there. Finished on the Eve of S. Andrew, 1929
OHMS
N
LONDON
THOU·ART·THE·FLOWER
OF·CITIES·ALL·
GREAT
WESTERN
RAILWAY
G.W.R. PADDINGTON STATION, LONDON, W.2.
PRINTED IN ENGLAND BY S.C. ALLEN & COMPANY LTD. 4 LISLE ST, LONDON, W.C.2.
JAMES MILNE, GENERAL MANAGER.

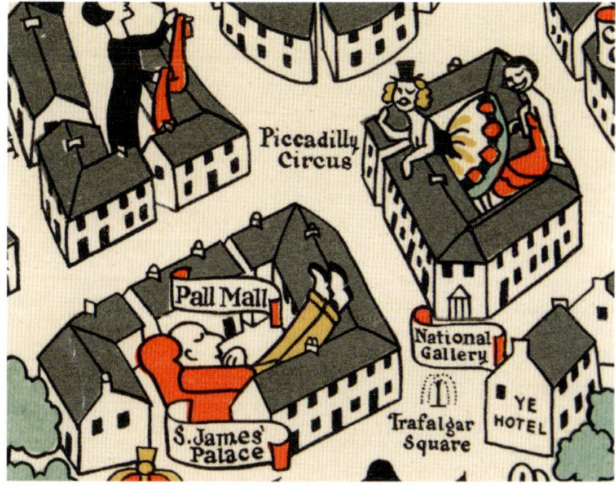

Opposite: *London Thou Art the Flower of Cities All*, Double Royal poster, 1929, 1016 x 635 mm

Above and right: Detail of *London Thou Art the Flower of Cities All*

She also designed a poster for Great Western Railway, *London Thou Art the Flower of Cities All*, a fabulous map encouraging people to come to London from the West and enjoy its delights (the title comes from a poem by William Dunbar, 'In Honour of the City of London'). She included some heraldry in the GWR poster, of course, as well as a lovely compass featuring a merman. Herry designed a poster for St Dunstan's (now Blind Veterans UK), too, to raise money for servicemen blinded in the First World War. People were encouraged to use a coach hired by St Dunstan's to go to the Derby, where St Dunstan's also organised the food and drink, and the profits went to help the blinded servicemen. Herry was photographed holding the poster, as seen in the June 1929 issue of *The Sphere* magazine, in an article entitled 'Women at Work: A Quintette of Distinguished Women in the Artistic and Commercial Worlds'.

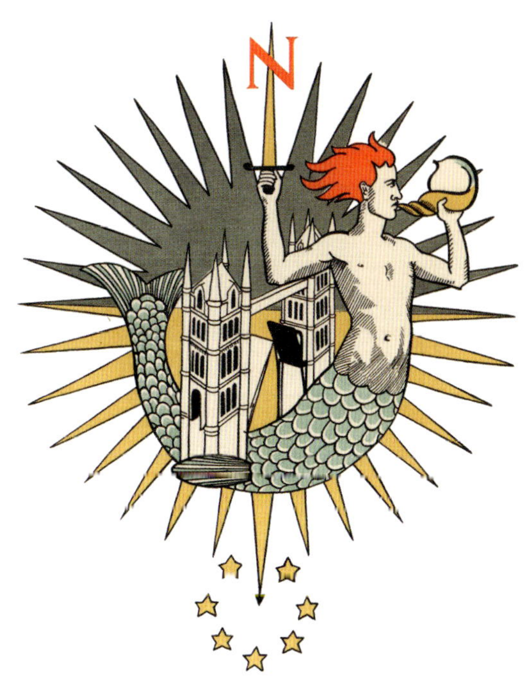

The year 1930 saw London Transport using another of Herry's poster designs to encourage people to use the bus network and go walking. All seven of the *Country Joys* series used exactly the same bucolic bird's-eye scene but with different lettering for each bus route; *Country Joys from Monument Station* is one of them. She also designed her first poster for a Lord's cricket test match, and she would go on to do others for this and other sporting events.

Meanwhile, Herry continued to do private commissions for maps. We will never be sure how many maps she did in her lifetime, but certainly many more than have been found; this is partly because some of the maps made as murals for houses were destroyed when they were redeveloped. In 1930 she was commissioned by William Walker, 1st Baron Wavertree (1856–1933), to do a map of the Japanese Garden at the National Stud thoroughbred horse-breeding facility near Kildare in Ireland. He was a keen breeder of racehorses and also an art collector (he bequeathed a large number of paintings to the Walker Art Gallery in Liverpool and his father had previously donated the building). No doubt he kept the original map, but in addition he had a process engraving made so that he could give copies to friends. She also designed a manuscript map for Captain and Mrs Abram Cottle, who were running a school at Ferney Hill near Wotton-under-Edge in the Cotswolds. Copies of it were presumably used to advertise the school and to tell people about its whereabouts and how to get there.

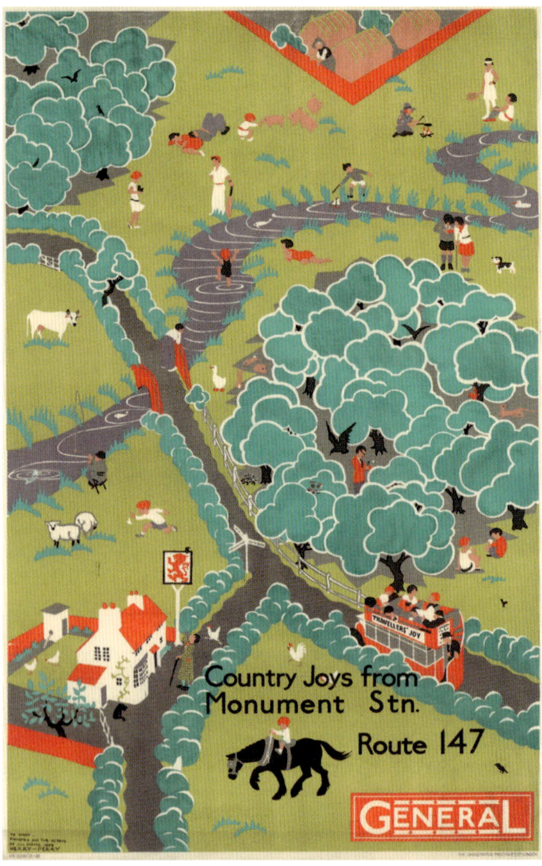

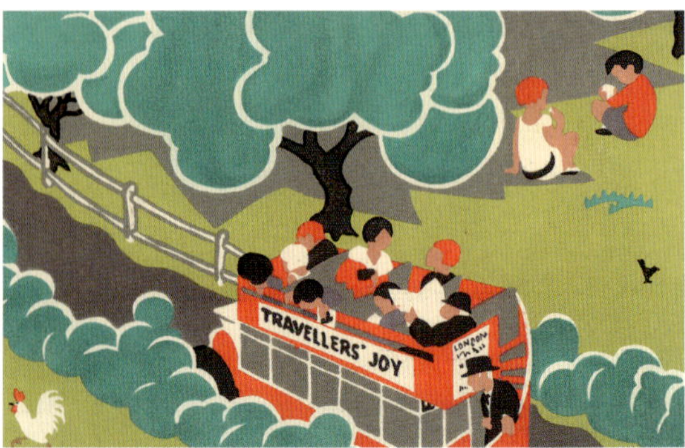

Above top: *Country Joys from Monument Station*, Double Royal poster, 1930, 1016 x 635 mm (© TfL from the London Transport Museum collection)

Above bottom: Detail from *Country Joys from Monument Station*

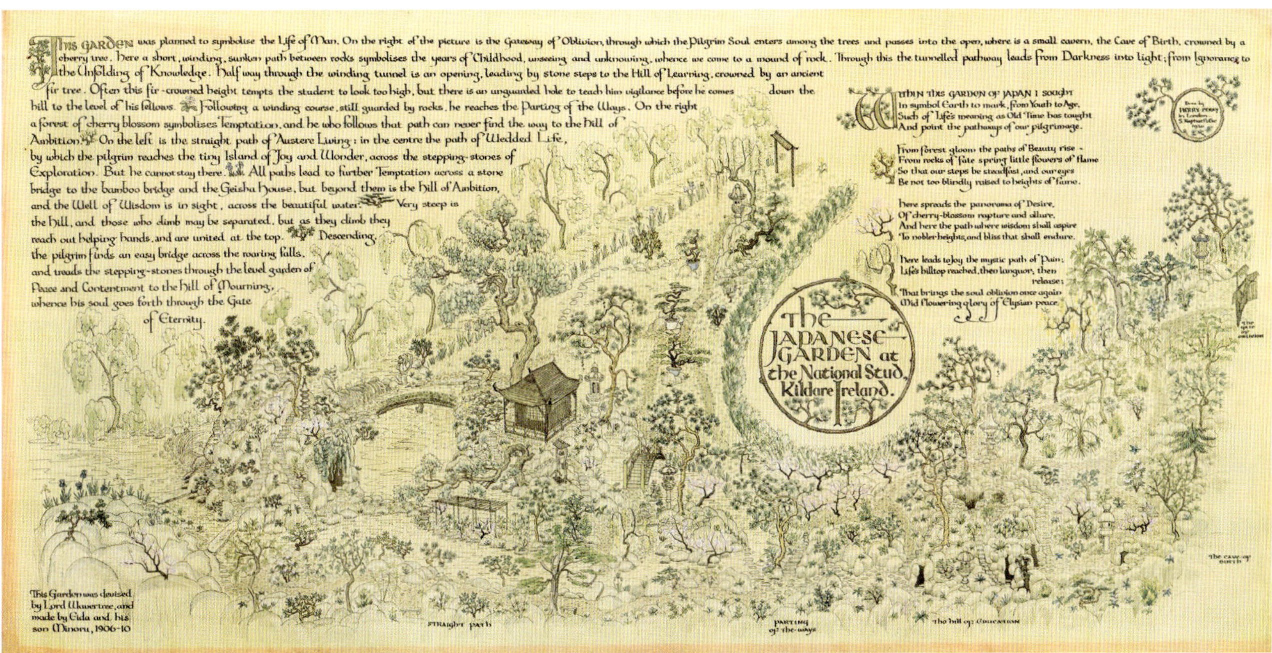

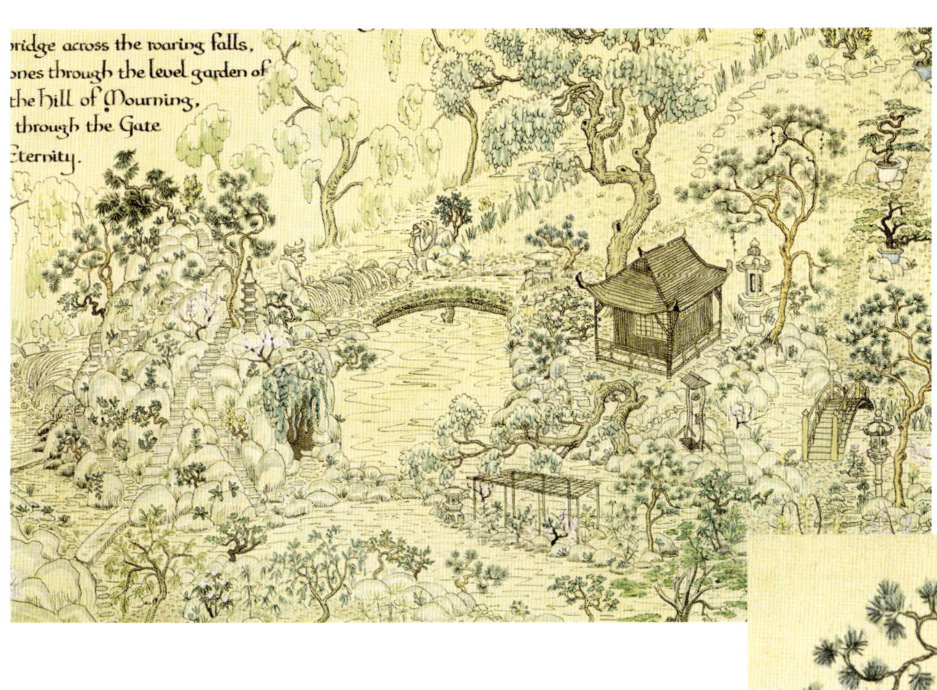

Above top: *The Japanese Garden at the National Stud, Kildare, Ireland*, process engraving, 1930, 390 x 760 mm

Above bottom and right: Details from *The Japanese Garden at the National Stud, Kildare, Ireland*

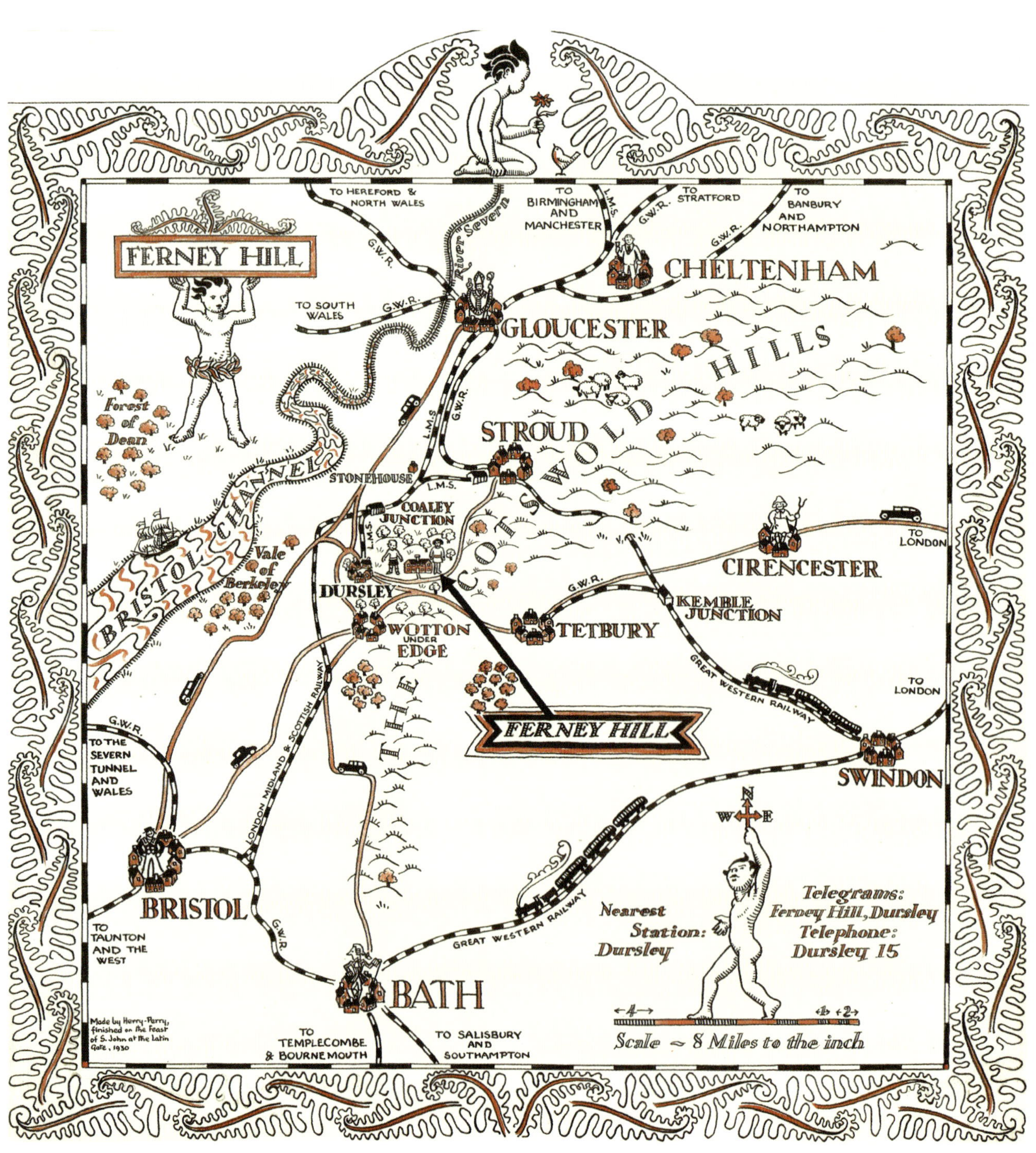

FERNEY HILL
TO HEREFORD & NORTH WALES
TO BIRMINGHAM AND MANCHESTER
TO STRATFORD
TO BANBURY AND NORTHAMPTON
L.M.S.
G.W.R.
G.W.R.
River Severn
G.W.R.
TO SOUTH WALES
G.W.R.
CHELTENHAM
GLOUCESTER
Forest of Dean
COTSWOLD HILLS
L.M.S.
G.W.R.
STROUD
STONEHOUSE
L.M.S.
BRISTOL CHANNEL
Vale of Berkeley
COALEY JUNCTION
L.M.S.
THE COTSWOLD
CIRENCESTER
TO LONDON
DURSLEY
G.W.R.
KEMBLE JUNCTION
WOTTON UNDER EDGE
TETBURY
FERNEY HILL
GREAT WESTERN RAILWAY
TO LONDON
THE
G.W.R.
TO THE SEVERN TUNNEL AND WALES
LONDON MIDLAND & SCOTTISH RAILWAY
SWINDON
N
W E
S
BRISTOL
GREAT WESTERN RAILWAY
Nearest Station: Dursley
Telegrams: Ferney Hill, Dursley
Telephone: Dursley 15
TO TAUNTON AND THE WEST
G.W.R.
BATH
Made by Herry-Perry, finished on the Feast of S. John at the Latin Gate, 1930
TO TEMPLECOMBE & BOURNEMOUTH
TO SALISBURY AND SOUTHAMPTON
4
2
Scale ~ 8 Miles to the inch

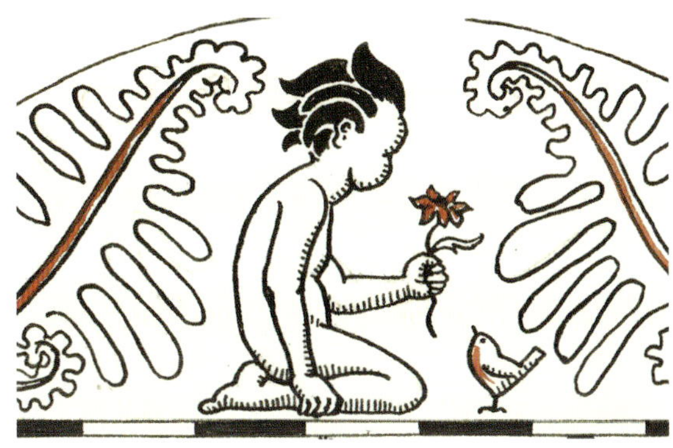

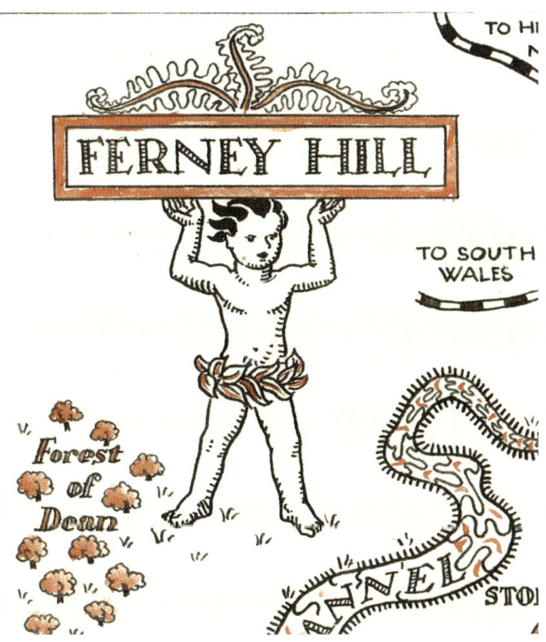

Another map design in 1930 was for Imperial and International Communications (better known these days as Cable & Wireless), following the creation of this company in 1929 to hold a monopoly interest in all the telegraphy companies around the British Empire. This world map showed all the company's radiotelegraphy stations, undersea cable network and cable ships. It may have been used as a mural at the company's headquarters in London, but the only remaining evidence of it is a 150-piece jigsaw puzzle which was used for promotional purposes. In 1945, MacDonald Gill (1884–1947) created a similar but more sophisticated map (in the form of a poster) for Cable & Wireless (*Cable & Wireless Great Circle Map*). Gill was the premier map artist of this time – and maybe any time – having designed his first map in 1909. It seems likely, because of their mutual interest in making maps, that Herry and Gill met, but there is no evidence for this, and there is no reference to her in the leading book on Gill by Caroline Walker.

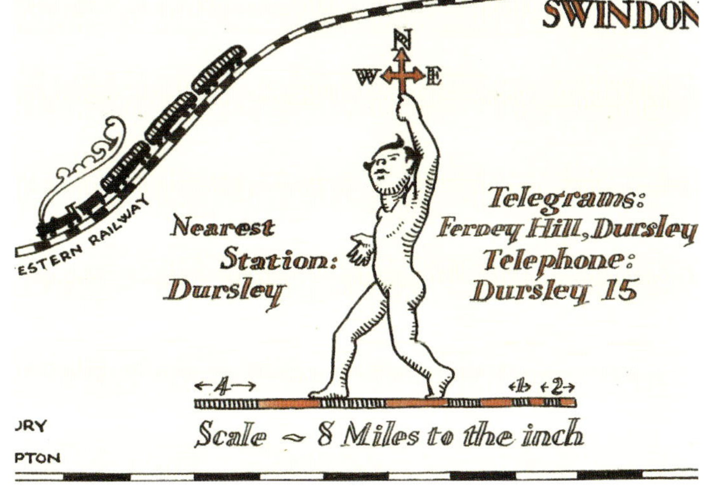

Opposite: The map of Ferney Hill, 1930, 353 x 320 mm

Above and right: Details from the map of Ferney Hill

Herry had a bumper year in 1931, producing 14 posters for London Transport. She now began to use a much more painterly style for some of her posters, as in the beautiful *Blackberry Time* and the somewhat saccharine *Bluebell Time*, *Crocus Time* and *Chestnut Sunday, Bushy Park*. These posters were designed to get people to use London Transport to visit the countryside and parks around London at various times of year.

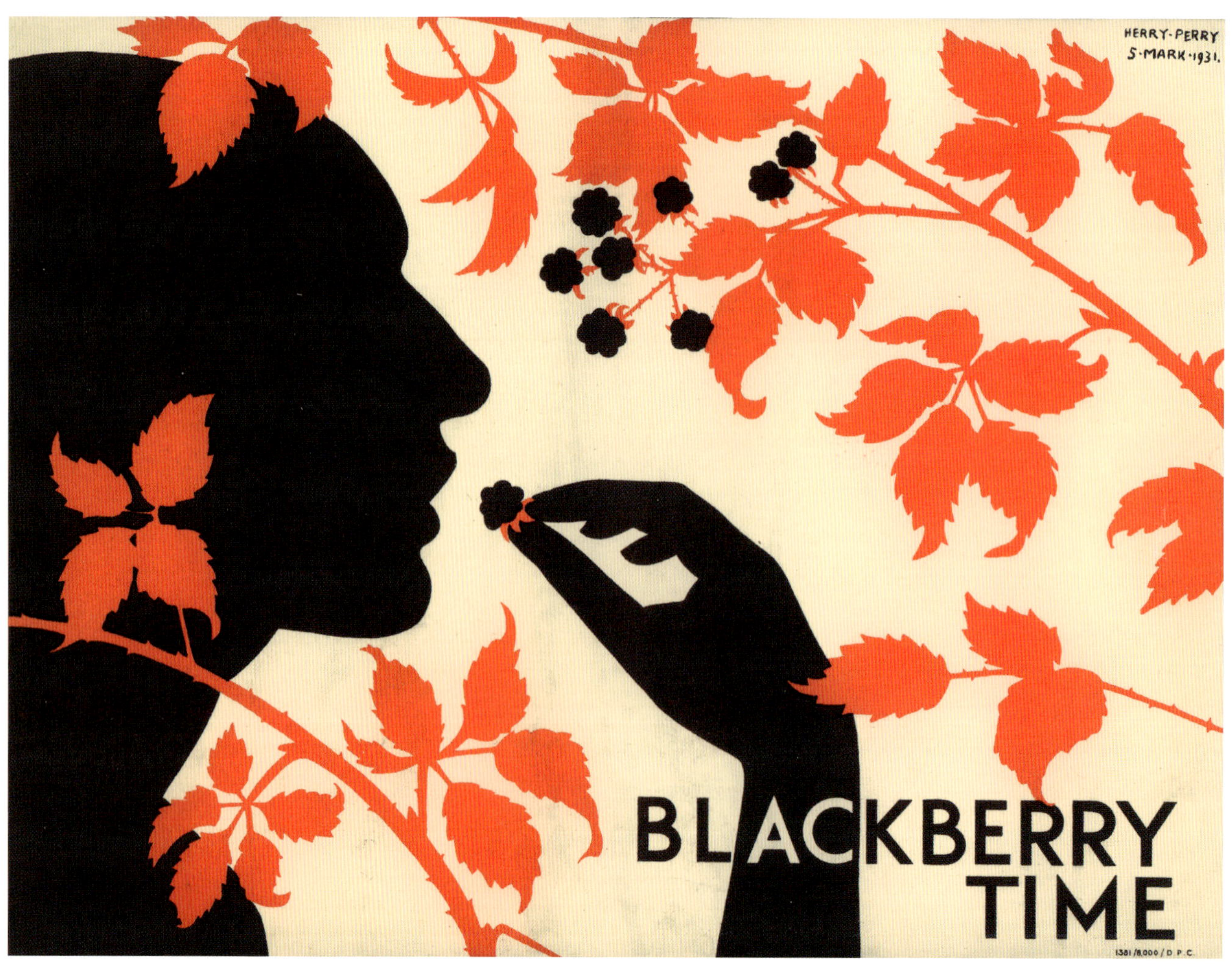

Above: *Blackberry Time*, poster, 1931, 255 x 330 mm (© TfL from the London Transport Museum collection)

Herry created some other clever posters, too, such as *Wimbledon*, with its unusual viewpoint from behind the ball boy, and the amusing *Derby Day*, with Herry appearing as a pigeon in a top hat with an artist's palette and paintbrush (a recurring theme – images of her as a pigeon in various hats occur in other posters).

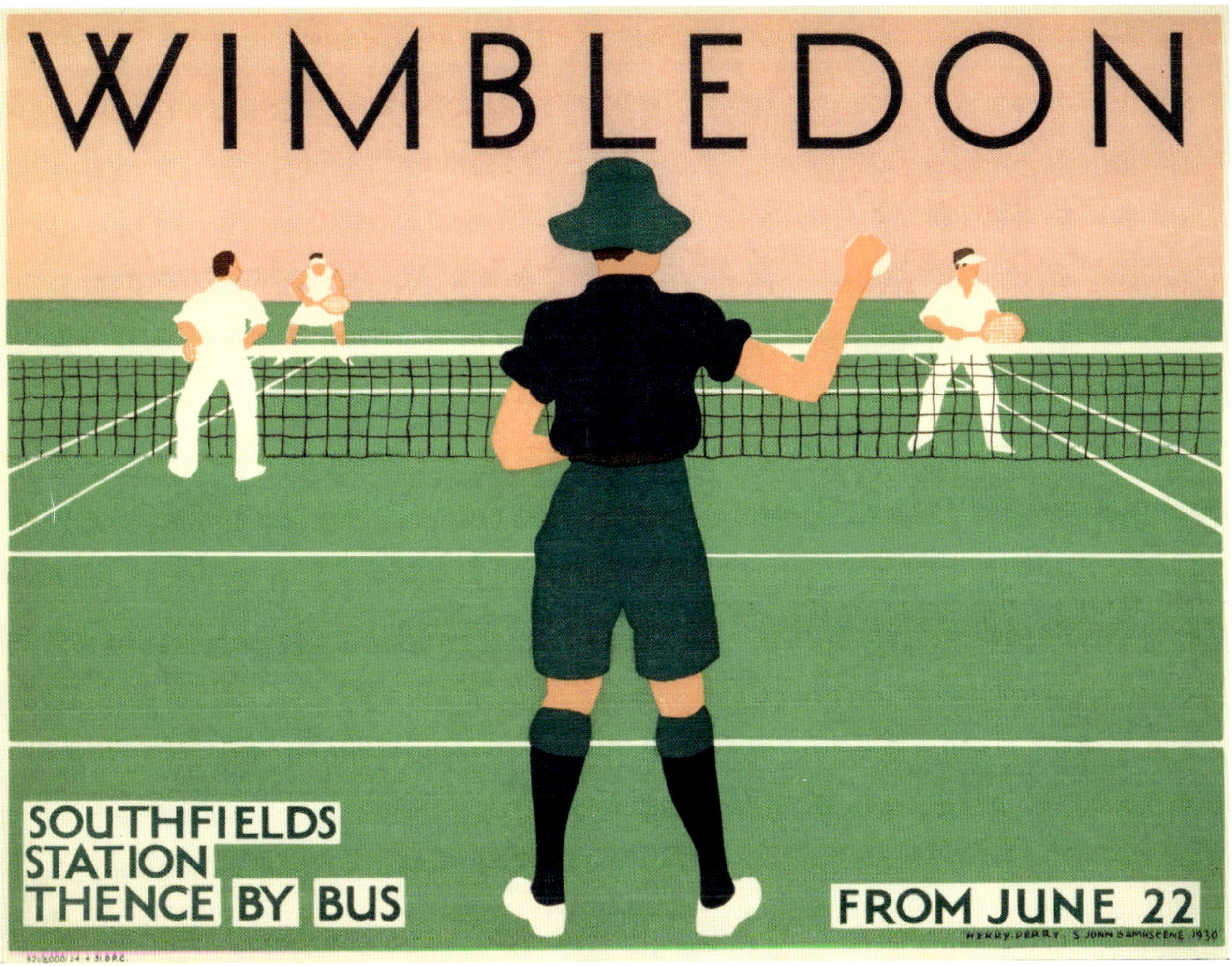

Above: *Wimbledon*, poster, 1931, 255 x 330 mm (© TfL from the London Transport Museum collection)

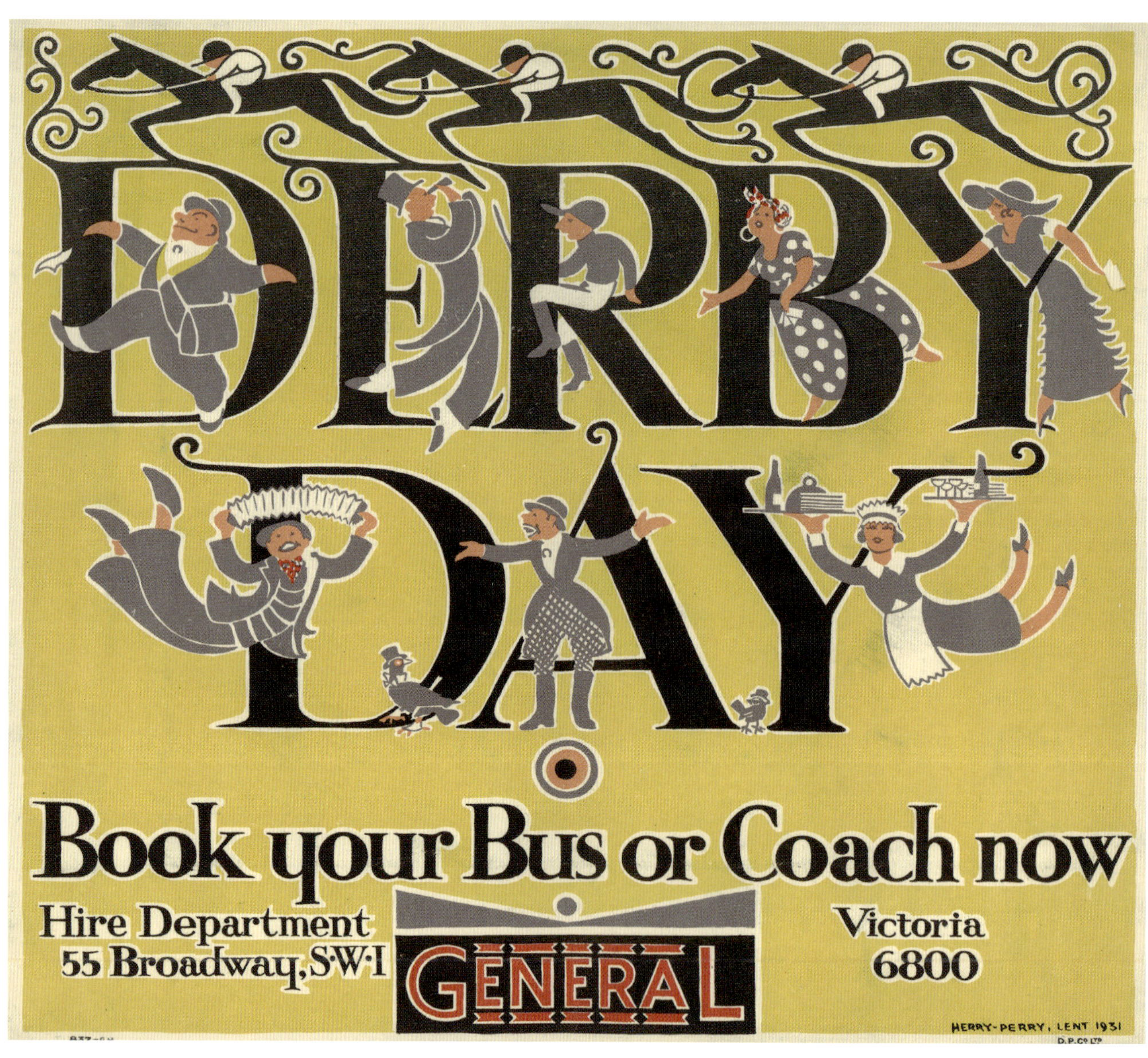

Above: *Derby Day*, poster, 1931, 298 x 330 mm
(© TfL from the London Transport Museum
collection)

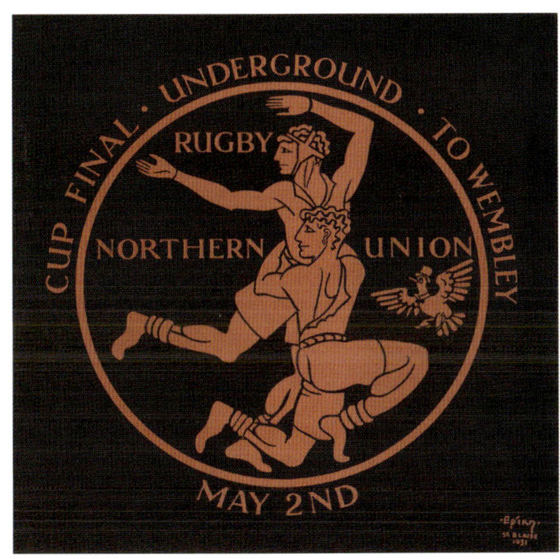

In 1931 there were two posters modelled on ancient Greek pottery, including *Rugby Northern Union Cup Final* (with Herry as a hatted pigeon again), as well as designs for two maps, although we don't know much about the maps. One was commissioned by Sir Julien Cahn, Ist Baronet (1882–1944), a wealthy businessman. It showed the Stanford Hall estate near Loughborough (now the Defence and National Rehabilitation Centre), which he owned. The other was a map of a fruit farm, said to have been commissioned by the Ministry of Agriculture. These were items 264 and 274 in the Arts and Crafts Exhibition Society's catalogue for its 1931 annual exhibition.

Above: *Rugby Northern Union Cup Final*, 1931, 305 x 305 mm (© TfL from the London Transport Museum collection)

Below: *Rugby League Cup Final,* poster, 1933, 255 x 330 mm (© TfL from the London Transport Museum collection)

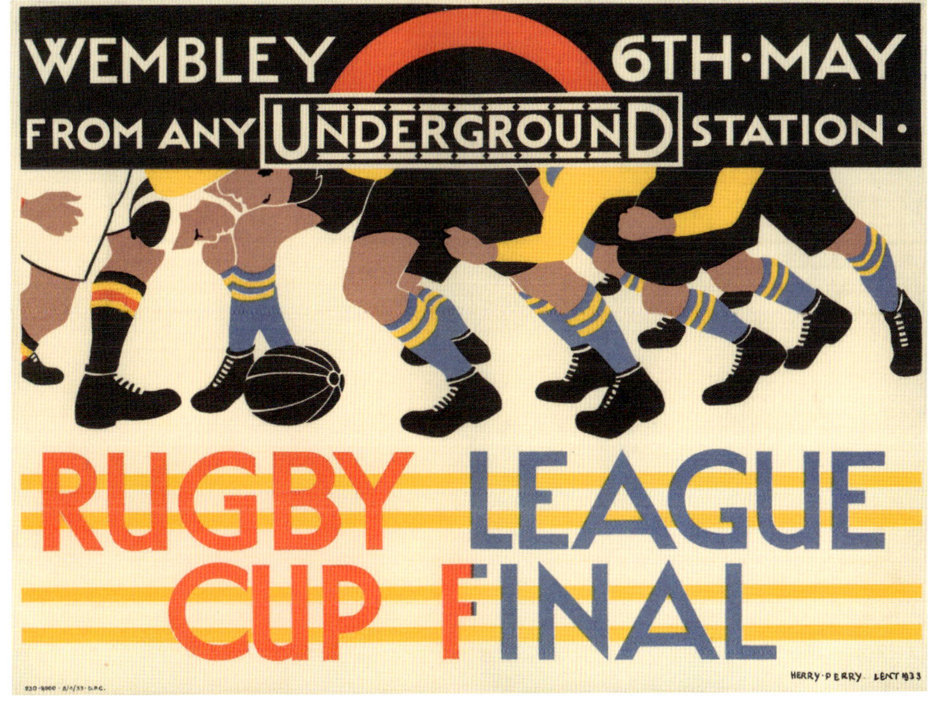

As most of her time in 1932 was spent doing the map mural at Rothamsted Experimental Station (see the 'Murals' section), it seems Herry had none left to do any posters. In 1933 and 1934, however, she did a total of nine posters for London Transport. These included three to promote rambling in the countryside and the associated guidebooks published by London Transport (including *800 Miles of Rambles*), and a series of four aimed at enticing visitors to travel to London that depicted people in historical costumes (such as *The Theatres*), as well as others like *Rugby League Cup Final*. The mural maps she designed for R.M.S. *Queen Mary* in 1934 are dealt with in 'Murals'.

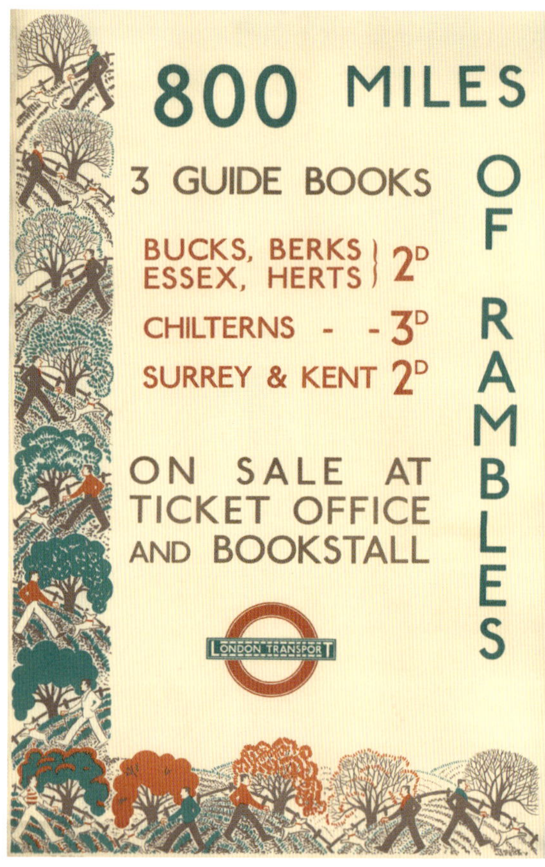

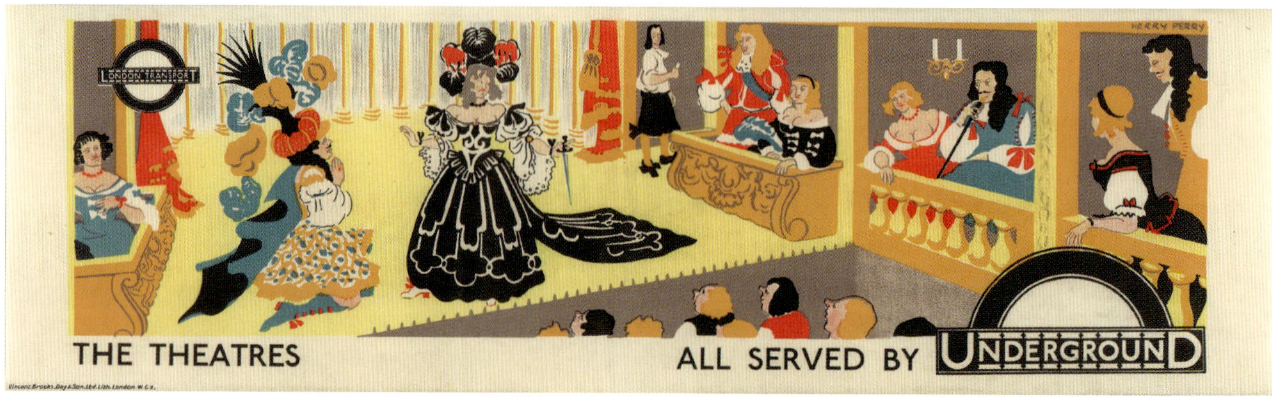

Above top: *800 Miles of Rambles*, Double Royal poster, 1934, 1016 x 635 mm (© TfL from the London Transport Museum collection)

Above bottom: *The Theatres,* poster, 1934, 204 x 654 mm (© TfL from the London Transport Museum collection)

Opposite top: *Derby Day*, poster, 1935, 254 x 317 mm (© TfL from the London Transport Museum collection)

Opposite bottom: *Lord Mayor's Show*, poster, 1935, 255 x 305 mm (© TfL from the London Transport Museum collection)

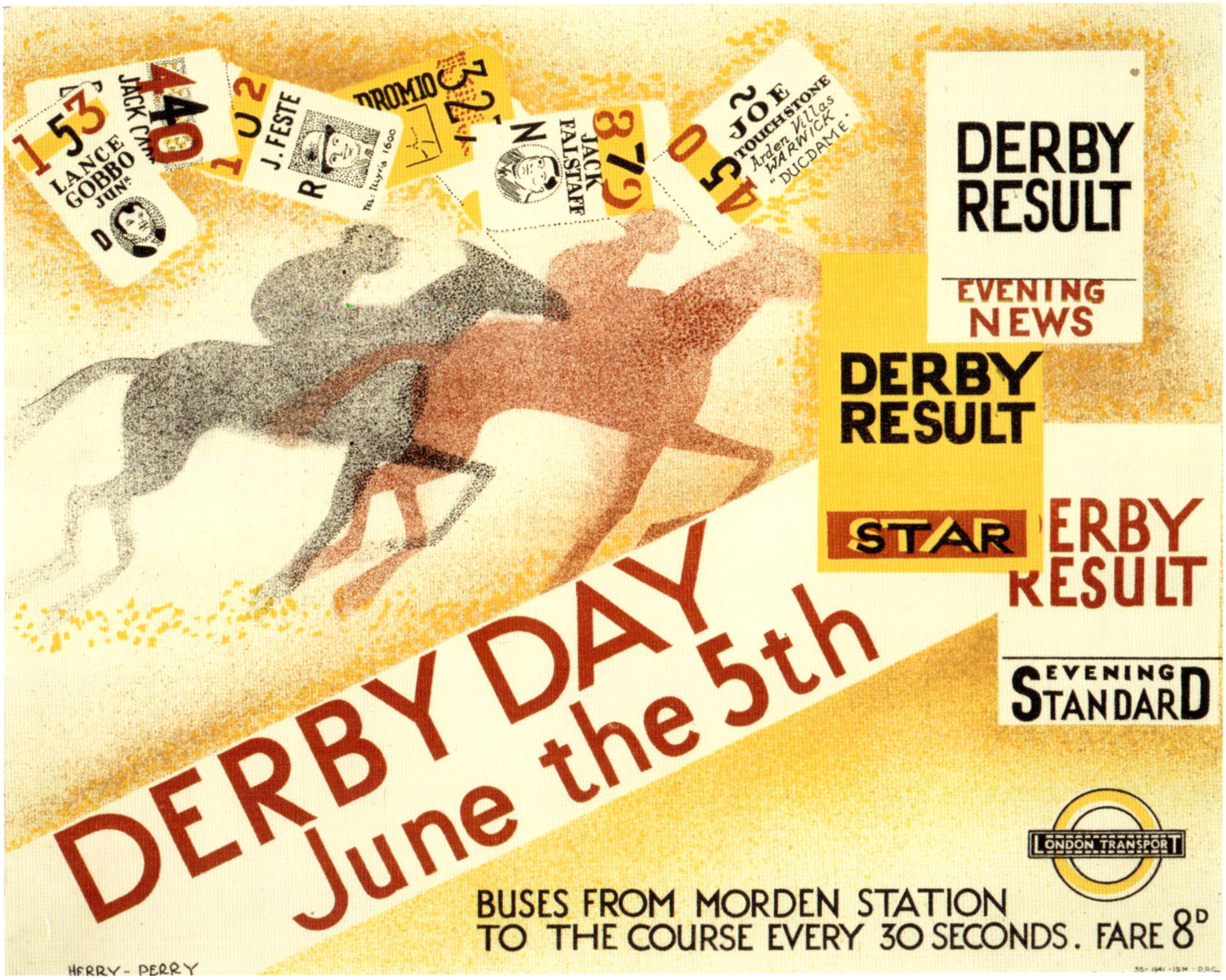

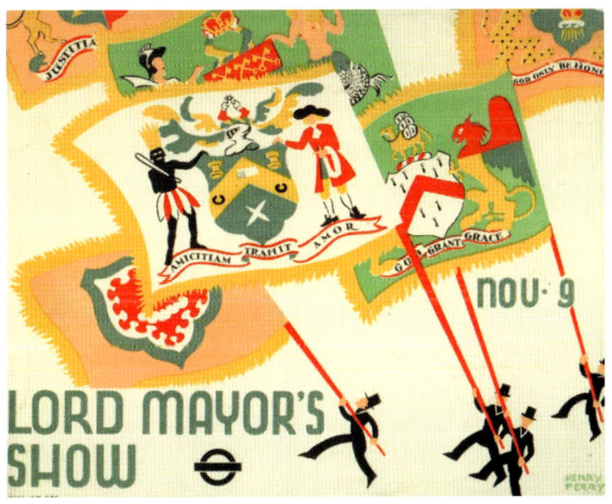

It was in 1935 that Herry reached her peak of poster-making, with 17 posters for London Transport. These included some of her best poster works, including a much more dynamic *Derby Day*, an imaginatively creative one of the *Cup Final* where the players are represented by collaged tickets, a *Lord Mayor's Show* with plenty of heraldry and an atmospheric *Boat Race*. There was, too, a poster for the International *Horse Show, Olympia* (showing a Nazi flag for the German team).

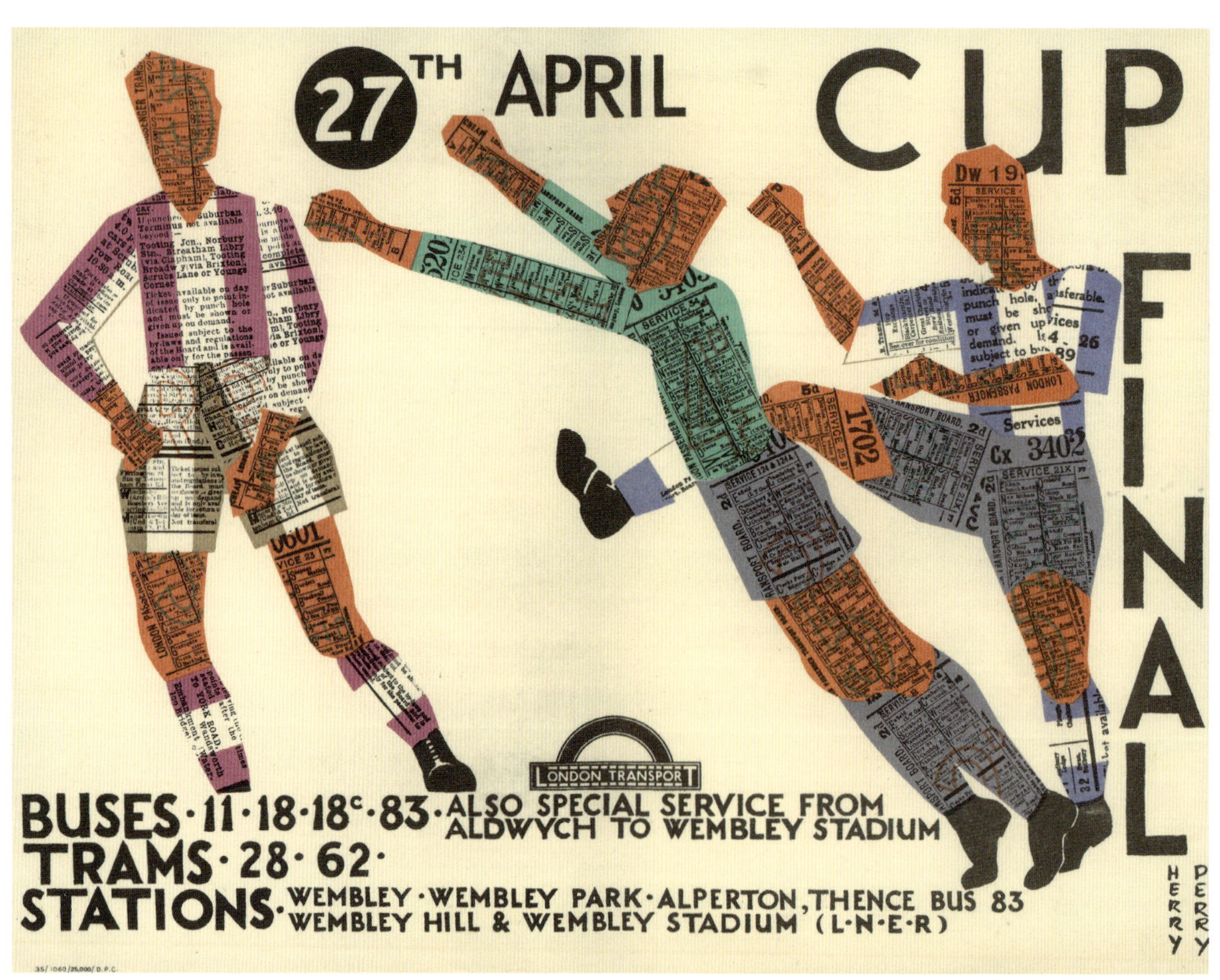

Above: *Cup Final*, poster, 1935, 255 x 318 mm
(© TfL from the London Transport Museum
collection)

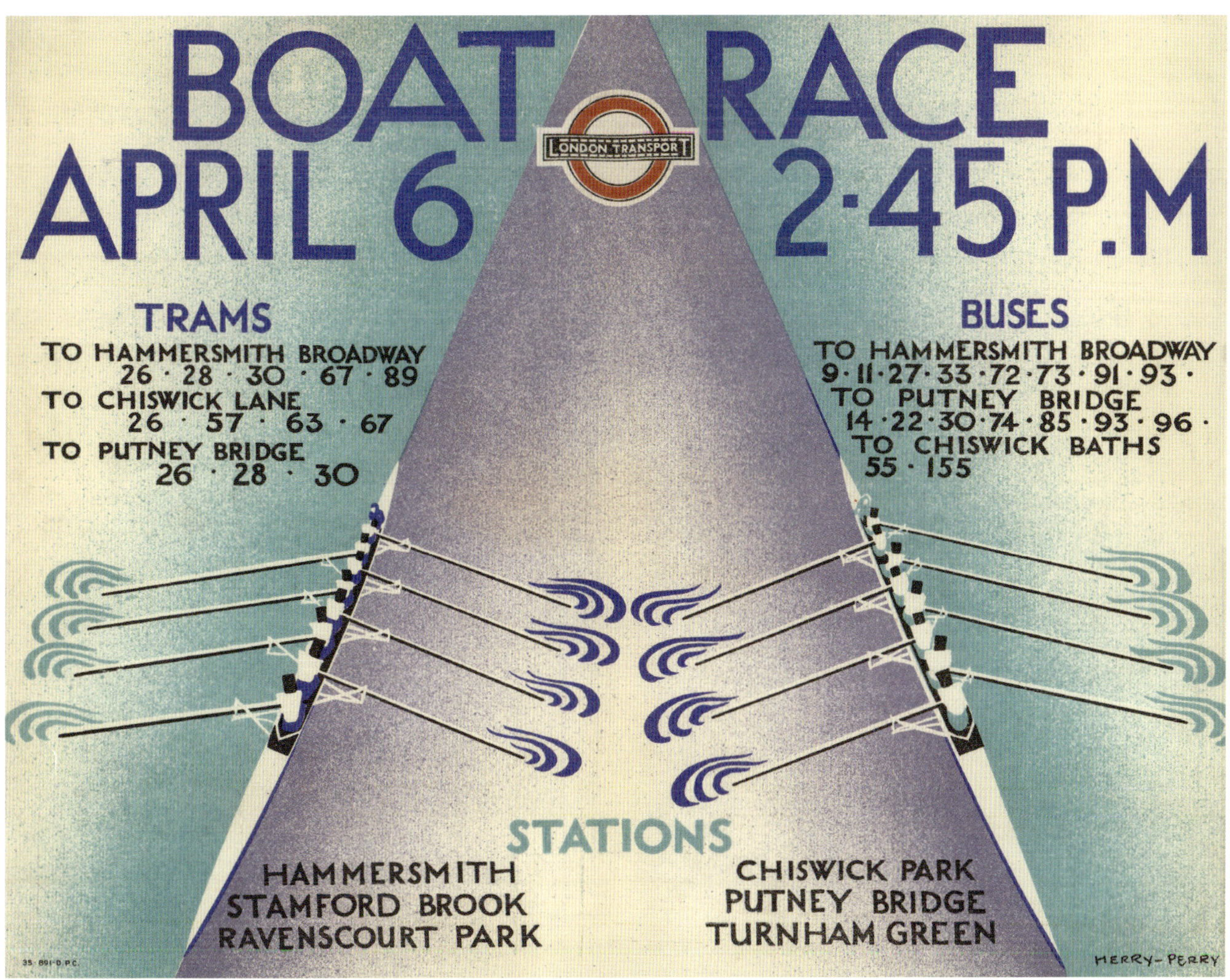

Above: *Boat Race*, poster, 1935, 255 x 318 mm
(© TfL from the London Transport Museum
collection)

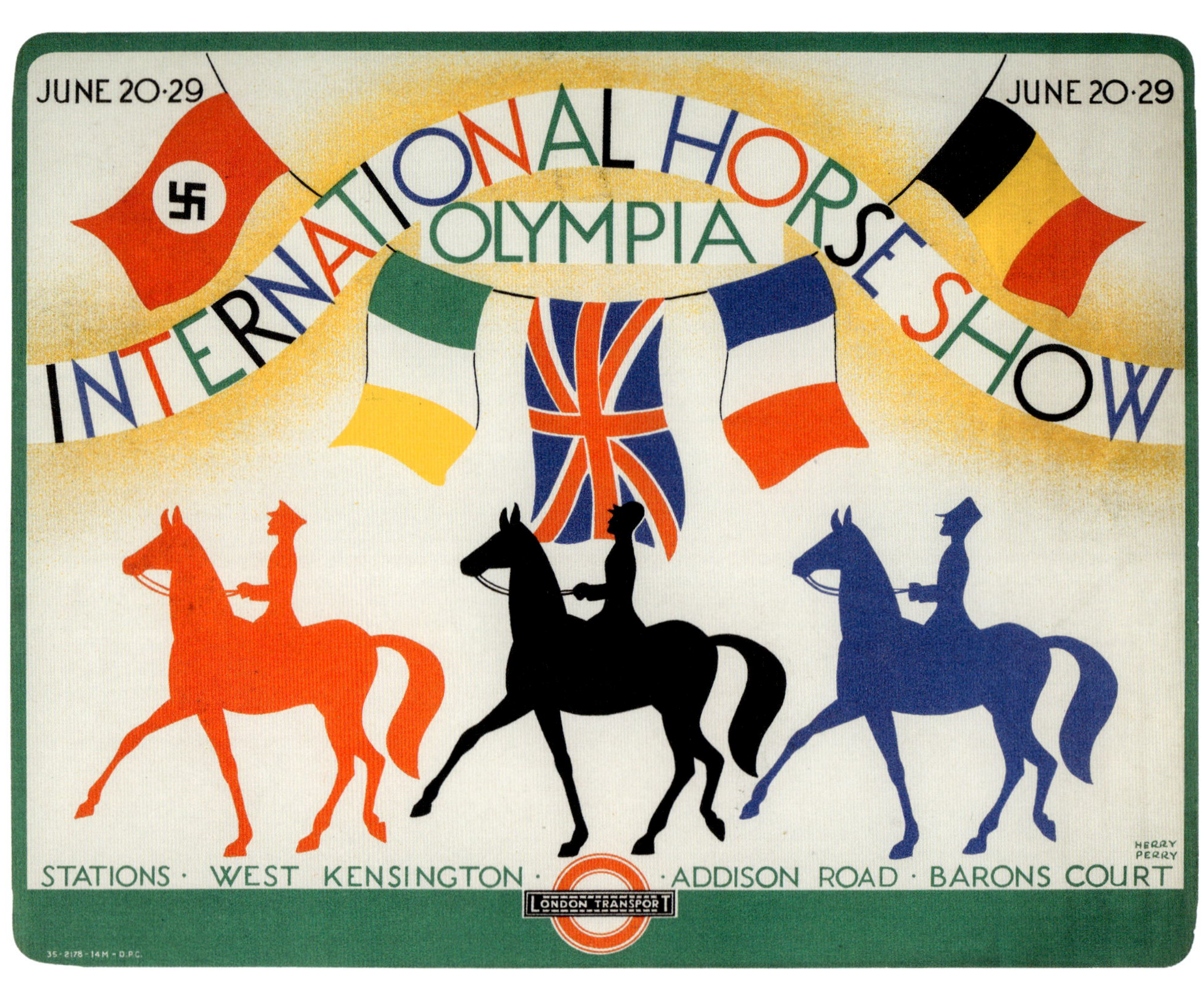

Above: *International Horse Show Olympia*, poster, 1935, 256 x 322 mm (© TfL from the London Transport Museum collection)

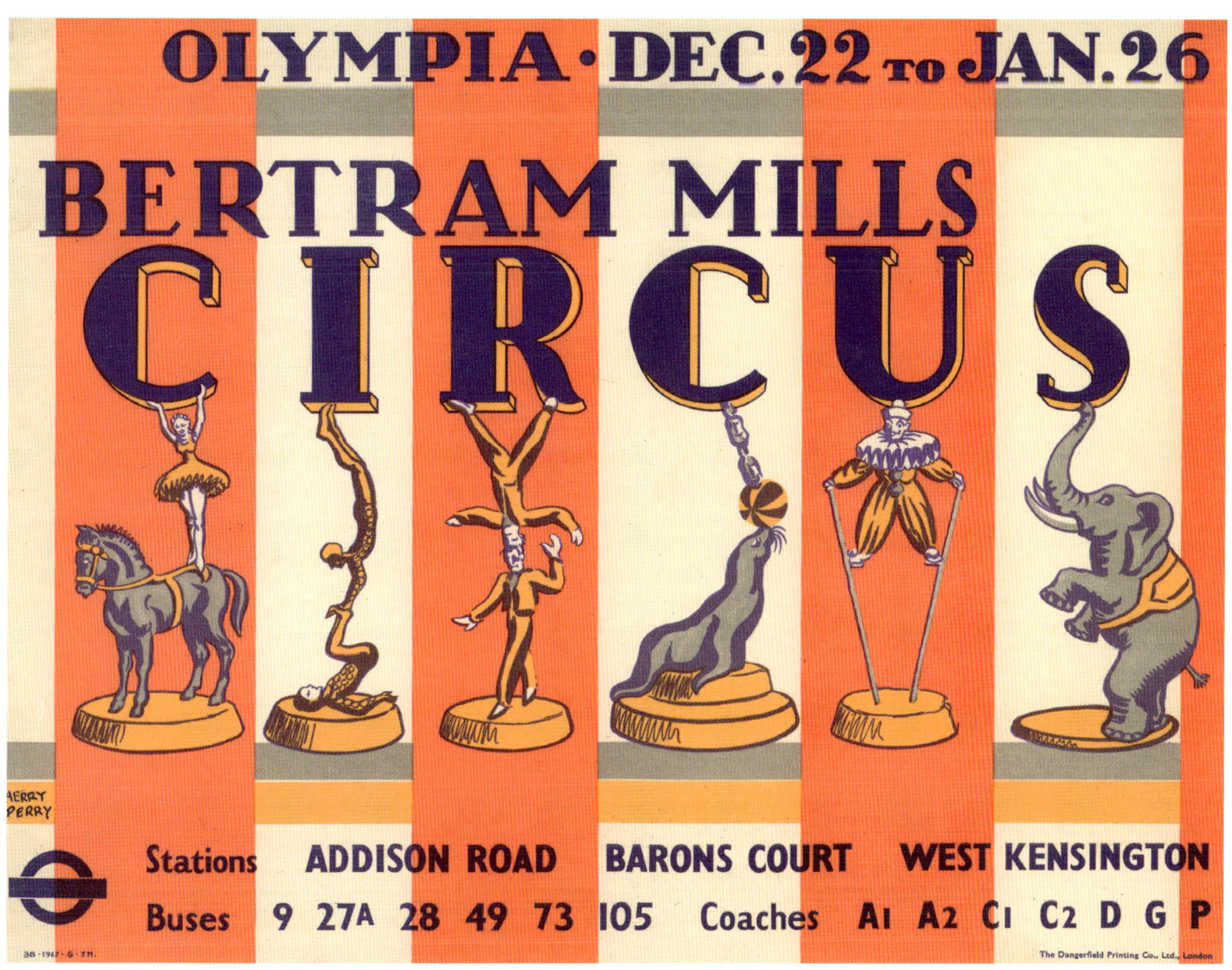

Above: *Bertram Mills Circus*, poster, 1938,
255 × 318 mm (© TfL from the London
Transport Museum collection)

As the map shows, Grosvenor House is in Park Lane—overlooking London's great garden, Hyde Park

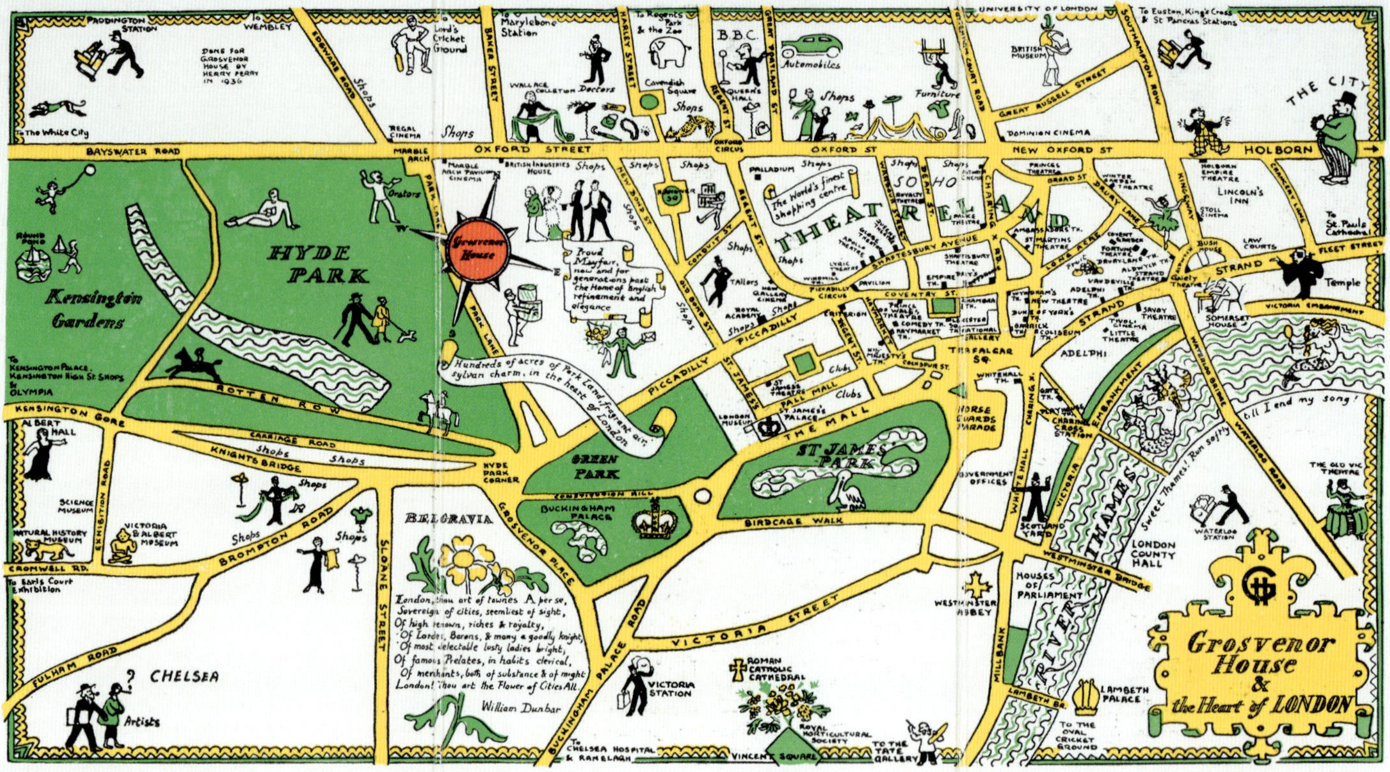

FASHIONABLE, CENTRAL *and* CHARMING

Whichever way you may enter London, wherever you may be in this great metropolis, Grosvenor House, in Park Lane, is easily reached.

The Hotel occupies three historic acres of the heart of London, and its commanding island site facilitates arrival and departure.

The wide-spreading greenery of Hyde Park pervades the air with sylvan charm and freshness—yet London's busy shops and crowded theatres are so near.

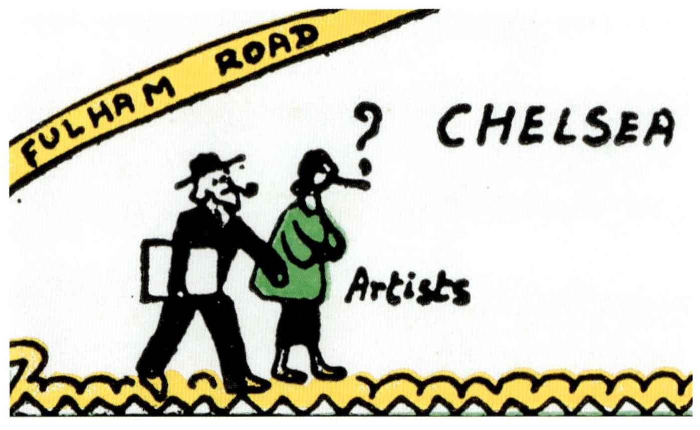

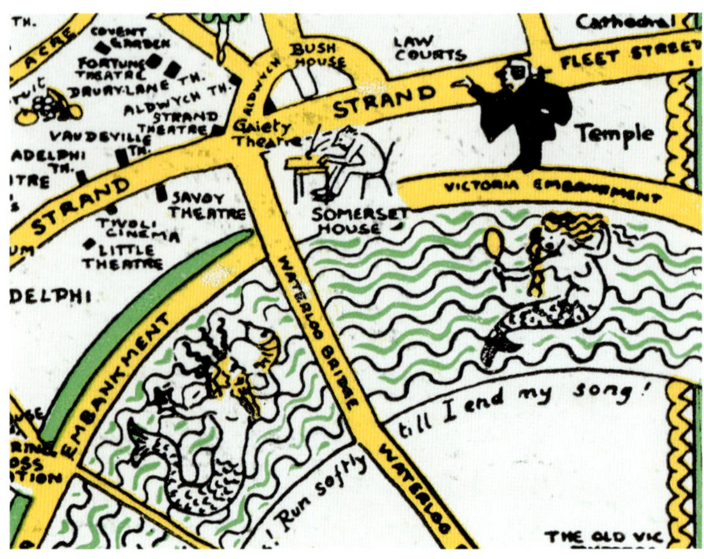

After 1935 Herry did a small map for the Grosvenor House hotel (c.1936), which was printed for customers to show them where the hotel was and the surrounding attractions and facilities. She also produced four more posters for London Transport in 1936–8, including *Bertram Mills Circus* (see page 65). The Second World War put an end to much of the advertising trade because of money and paper shortages, plus Frank Pick left London Transport in 1940 and died in 1941. Herry did not return to making maps or posters after the war.

Opposite top: The map for the Grosvenor House hotel, Park Lane, London, c.1936, 220 x 300 mm

Opposite bottom and below: Details from the map for the Grosvenor House hotel, Park Lane, London

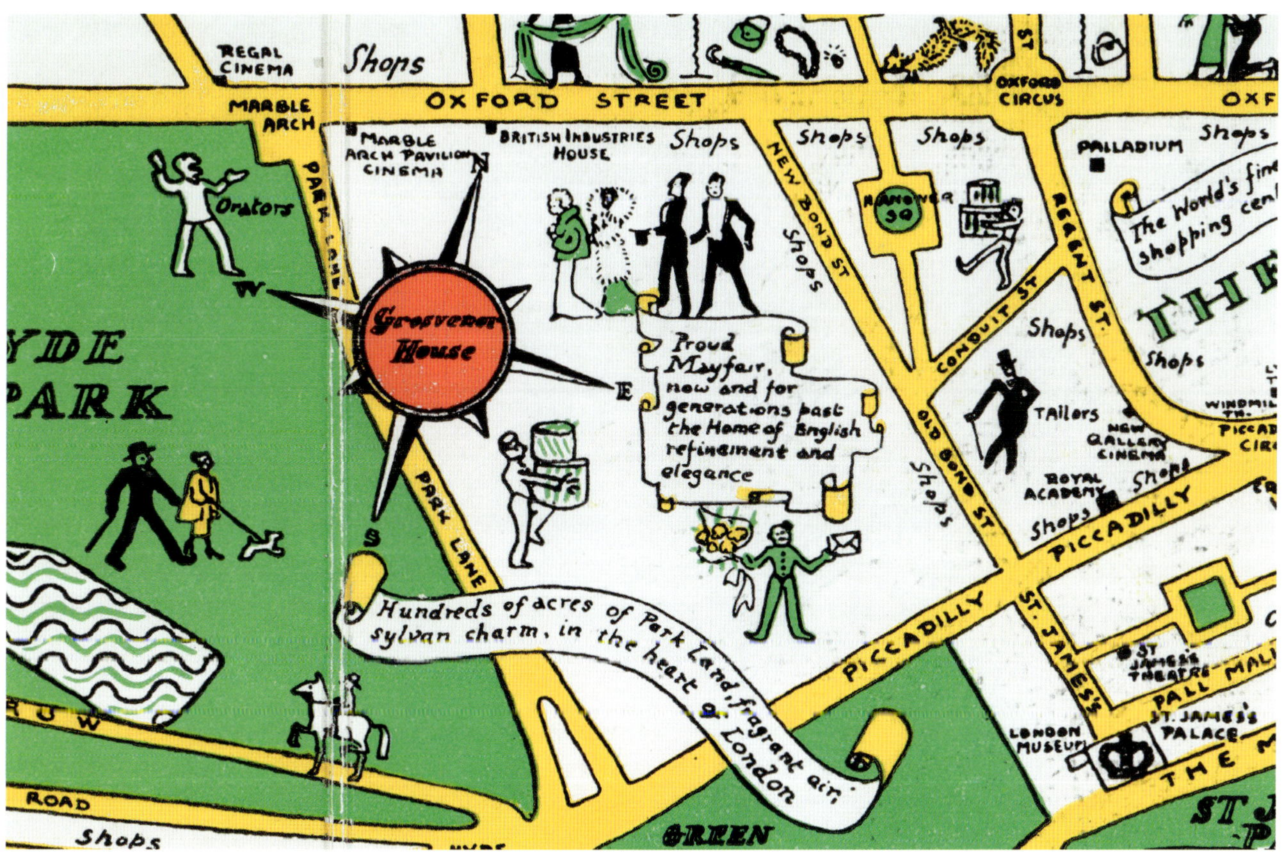

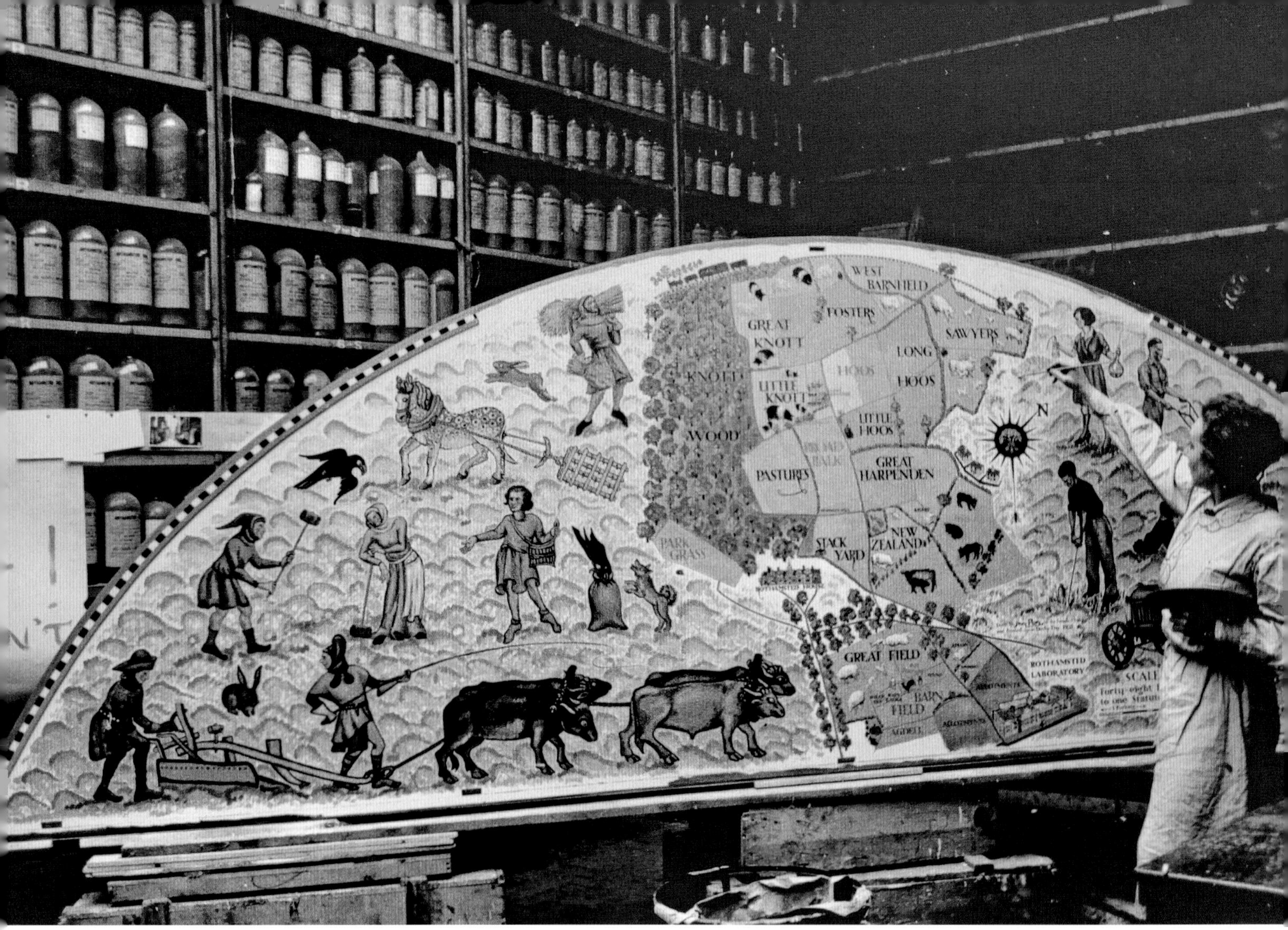

WEST BARNFIELD
FOSTERS
GREAT KNOTT
SAWYERS
LONG HOOS
KNOTT
HOOS
LITTLE KNOTT
LITTLE HOOS
WOOD
PASTURES
GREAT HARPENDEN
PARK GRASS
STACK YARD
NEW ZEALAND
N
GREAT FIELD
BARN FIELD
ROTHAMSTED LABORATORY
SCALE
Forty-eight to one Statute

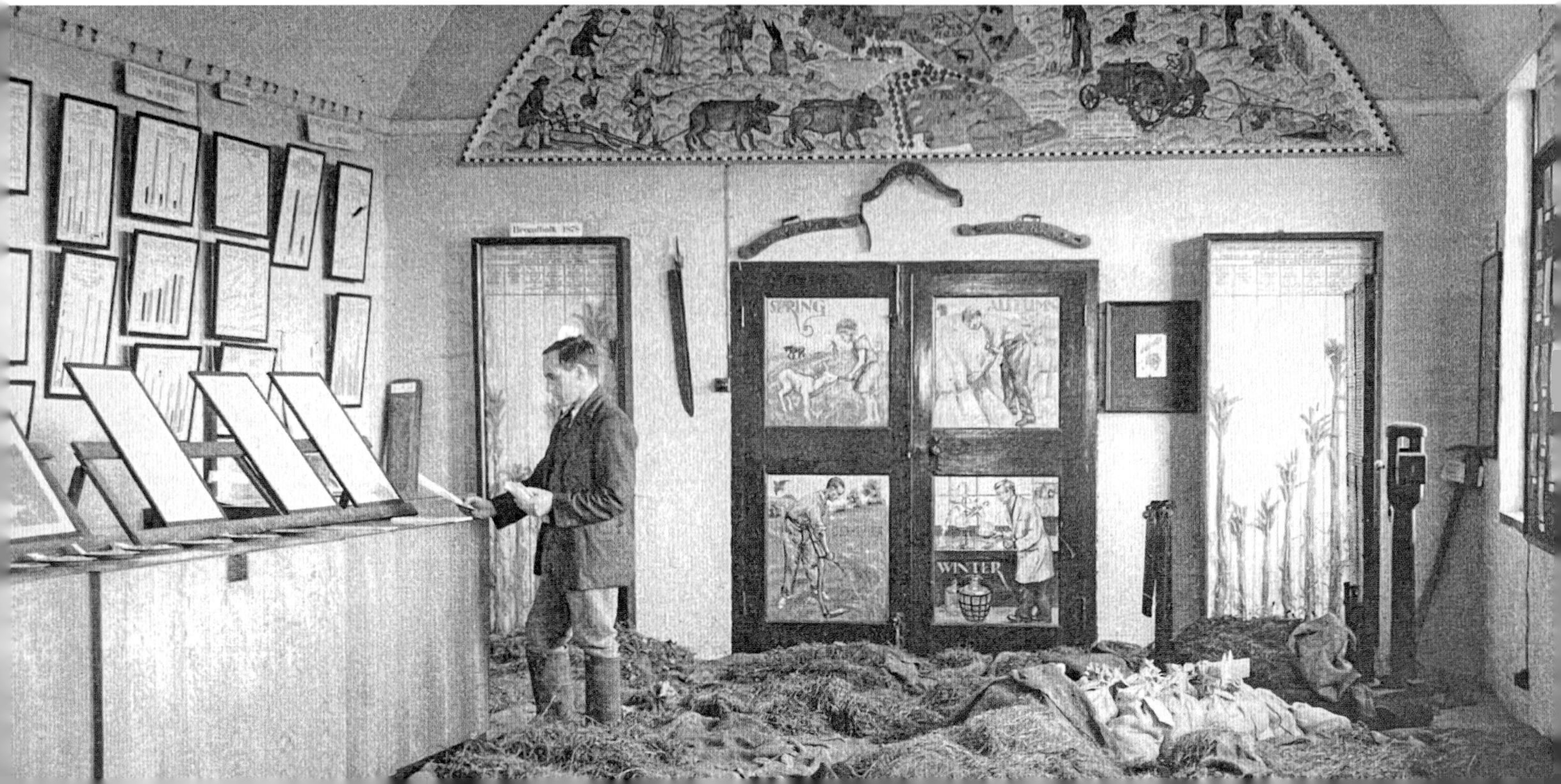

SPRING
AUTUMN
WINTER

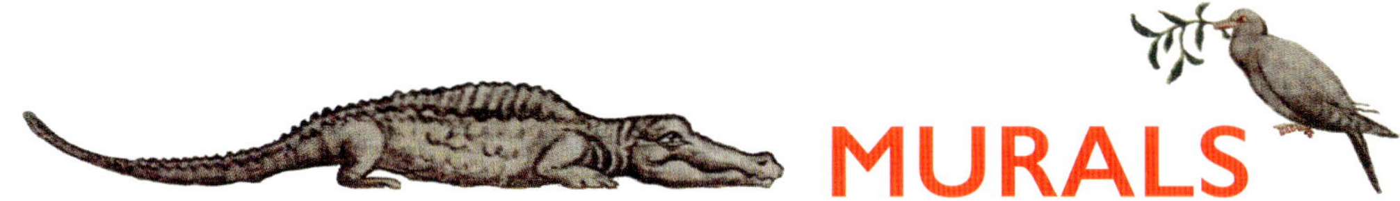

MURALS

Murals were a very popular art form in the 1920s and '30s. Companies and rich private individuals commissioned murals for their headquarters, homes and ships. Many have been lost over the years as buildings were demolished or redecorated or ships were scrapped. The two leading books on British murals in the twentieth century (see Selected Bibliography) give excellent overviews of the artists involved, but Herry doesn't get a mention. Nor was she included in 'Mural Painting in Great Britain 1919–1939', an exhibition of photographs of murals at the Tate Gallery in 1939. However, Herry was involved in designing two murals we know about and certainly did a few others (see the 'Maps and Posters' section).

In 1932, Herry was commissioned to paint a mural for the Rothamsted Experimental Station (now Rothamsted Research), an agricultural research facility in Harpenden, Hertfordshire. We are lucky that the mural has been well looked after there and the correspondence in relation to the commission has been preserved in their library. The

Opposite top: Herry Perry painting the mural for Rothamsted Experimental Station in the Old Sample House, 1932 (© Rothamsted Research (Rothamsted Library archive RUS 2.7))

Opposite bottom: The mural and the four panels in the Demonstration Room at Rothamsted Experimental Station, 1930s (© Rothamsted Research (Rothamsted Library archive RUS 2.7))

Director of Rothamsted at the time, Sir John Russell, was keen to have a map of the station's farm and buildings that properly reflected Rothamsted's research work. The proposal was to put the map in the newly built Demonstration Room, where farmers were told about Rothamsted's research work and were shown soil and crop samples, especially on wet days when such things couldn't be done outside in the fields.

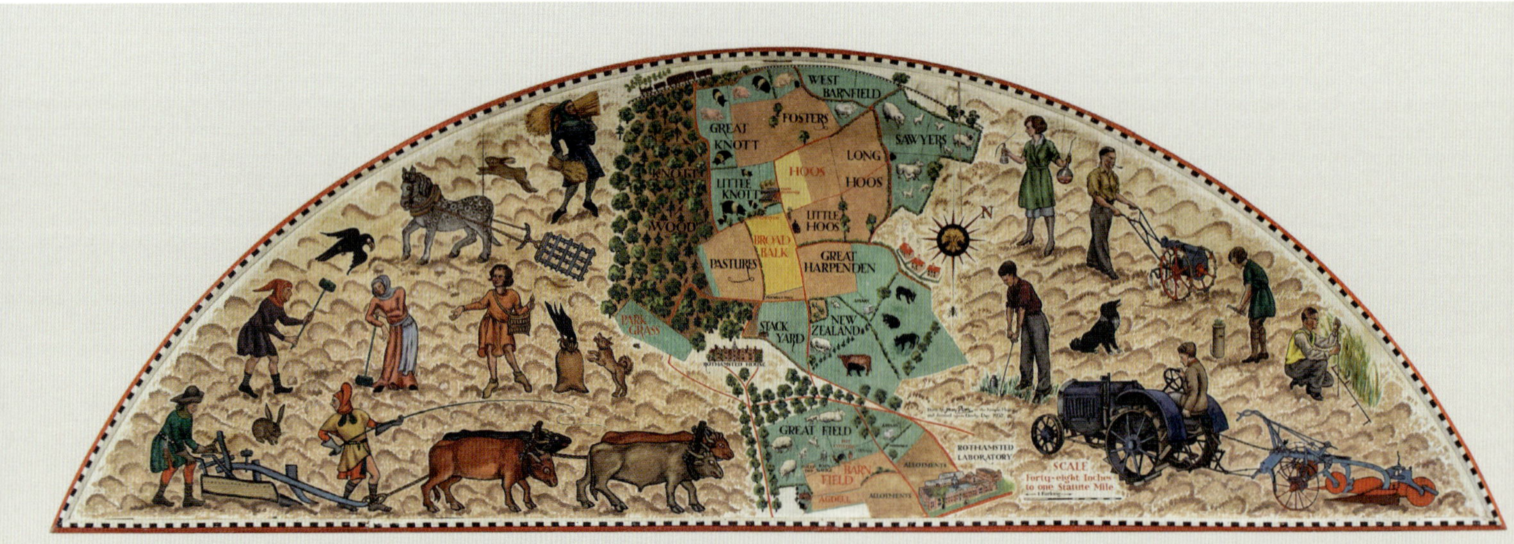

Sir John started his search for an artist in early 1931, seeking advice from the Empire Marketing Board about possible artists to use. An initial suggestion was MacDonald Gill (see the 'Maps and Posters' section), but his 150 guineas quotation was too expensive. In March 1932 Rothamsted wrote to Herry asking whether she would be interested in doing a map in a style similar to MacDonald Gill's *Highways of Empire* map (1927). Herry quickly agreed and it was decided she would paint it in

Above: The mural at Rothamsted in 2024 (© Rothamsted Research (Rothamsted Library archive RUS 2.7))

Opposite: Details from the mural at Rothamsted

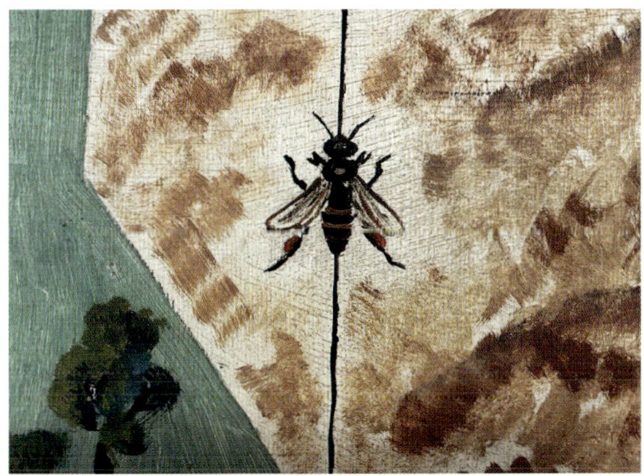

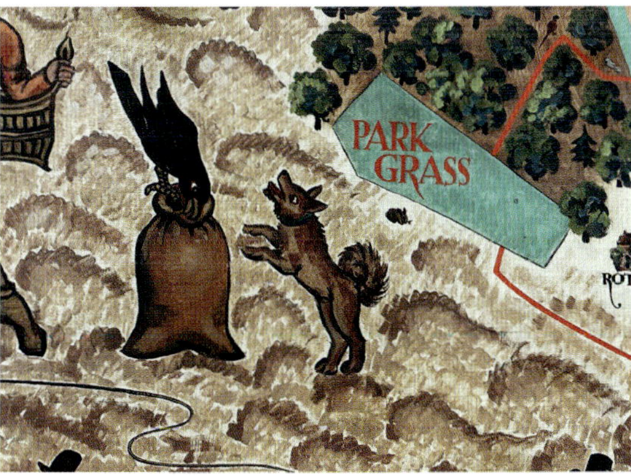

oils on plywood in a lunette (half-moon) shape for a fee of £50 (about £2,900 today) plus the cost of materials. She sent photographs of previous maps she had done and they agreed in early April to base the Rothamsted commission on the map she had painted for Sir Julien Cahn Bt at Stanford Hall, Loughborough (see the 'Maps and Posters' section).

The Rothamsted map was finished on 1 June. From correspondence we know that Herry enjoyed this commission and got on well with Sir John and Lady Russell, as well as other members of the staff (she did pencil portraits of Sir John and one of the staff – Dr Frederick Tattersfield – as well as a Christmas card for the Station in 1932). There is an amusing photograph showing Herry painting the mural in the Old Sample House, surrounded by bottles full of soil and with a sign warning people to keep their hands off the mural! (see page 68) The mural shows the farm and contrasts medieval and modern methods of farming. Some amusing vignettes include an angry rook, an insect hanging off the compass, and a dog barking at a thieving rook. There is a photograph of the mural installed above the door in the Demonstration Room with what look like hay or straw samples on the floor. On the door beneath the mural are four panels depicting the four seasons on the farm and in the laboratory, painted by Herry at some point after the mural. There is no correspondence relating to the panels but I suspect they were done in 1933.

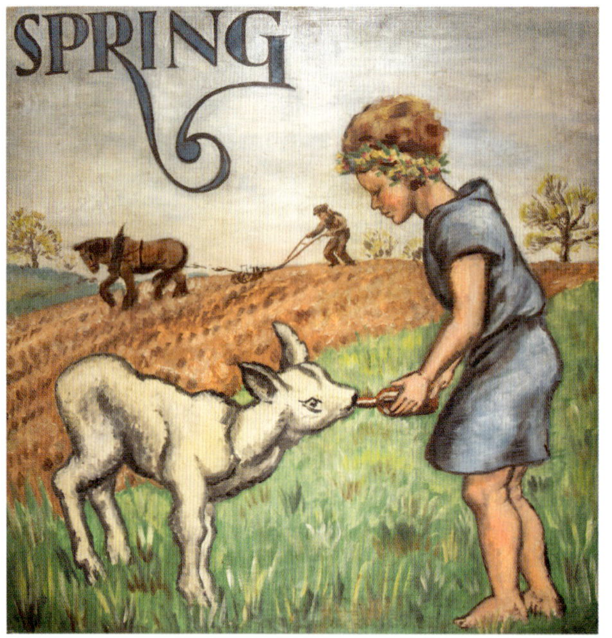

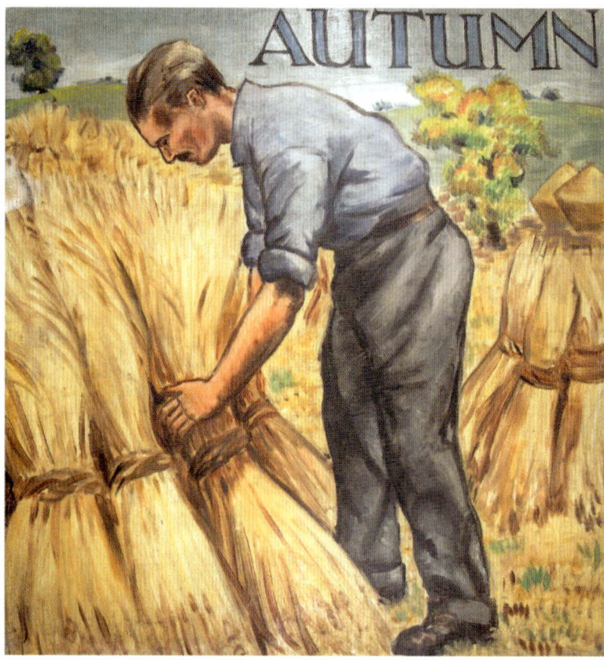

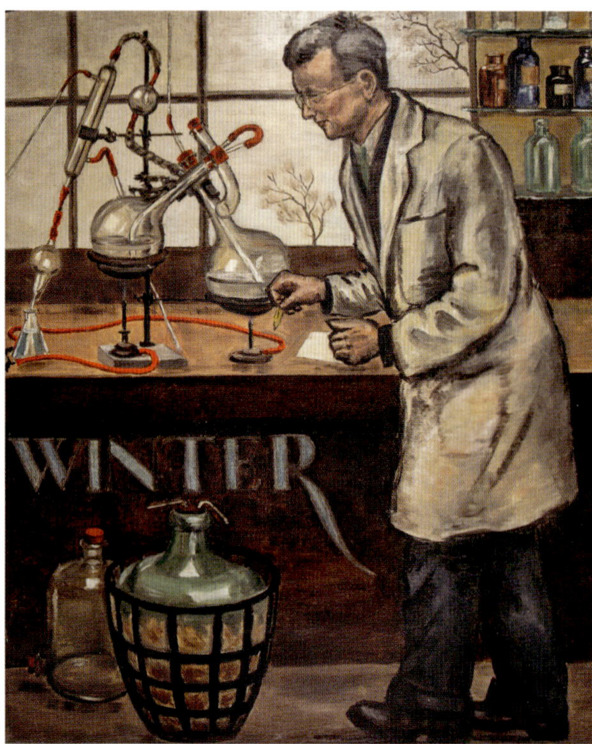

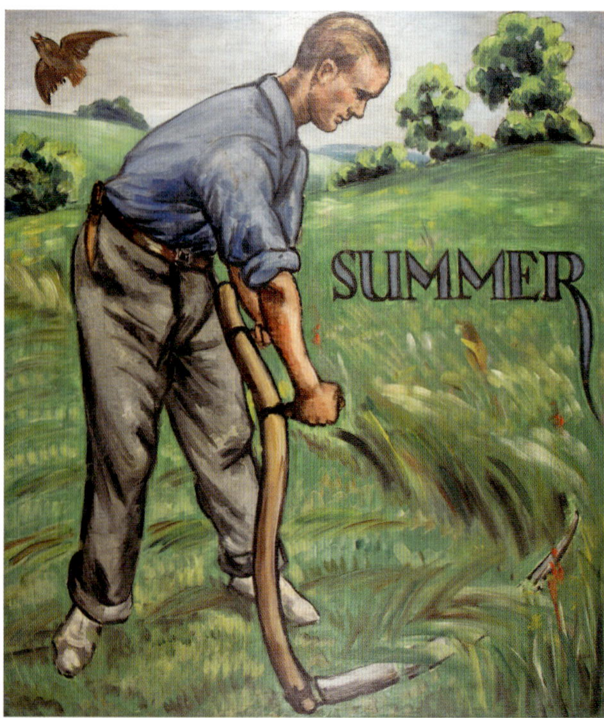

Above: The four panels at Rothamsted in 2024
(© Rothamsted Research (Rothamsted Library
archive RUS 2.7))

Another mural commission involved the R.M.S. *Queen Mary*, which was launched in September 1934 and had her maiden voyage in May 1936. Between those dates a huge project was carried out to decorate the interior of the liner using some of the leading artists of the day: MacDonald Gill (of course), Dame Laura Knight, Maurice Lambert, Edward Wadsworth and Anna and Doris Zinkeisen, to name but a few. As part of this, Herry was commissioned to do two pieces. The first was a mural on the theme of Noah's Ark for the Second-Class Children's Playroom and some wooden toys for the children to play with. Luckily, we have a number of photographs of Herry painting the mural (from late 1935/early 1936) and of the completed Playroom. As usual there are some amusing features, such as the telegraph wire strung along the top of the ark. Below the ark there was a blackboard for the children to draw on.

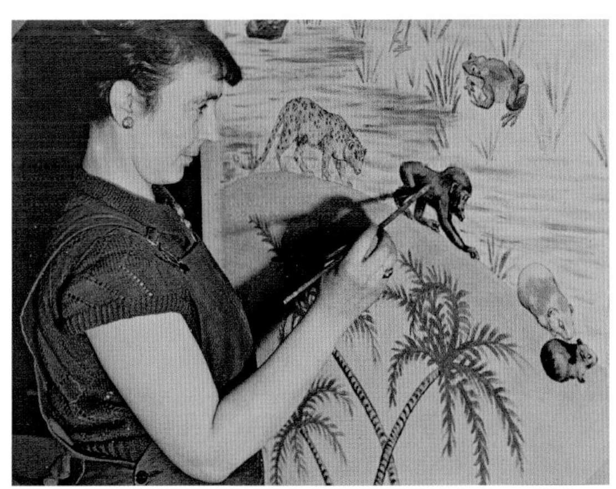

Above and below: Herry Perry painting her mural of Noah's ark for R.M.S. *Queen Mary* in late 1935/early 1936

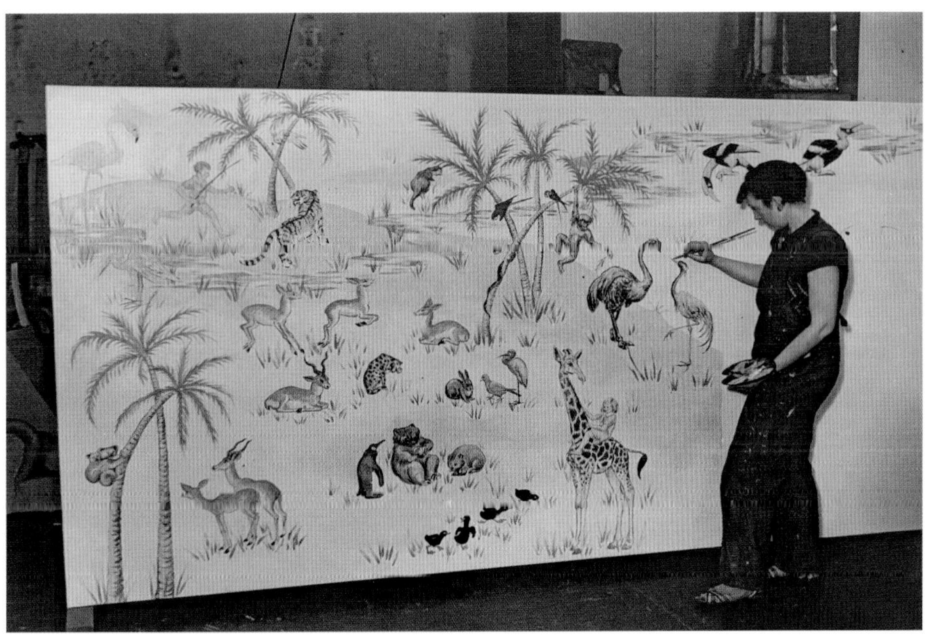

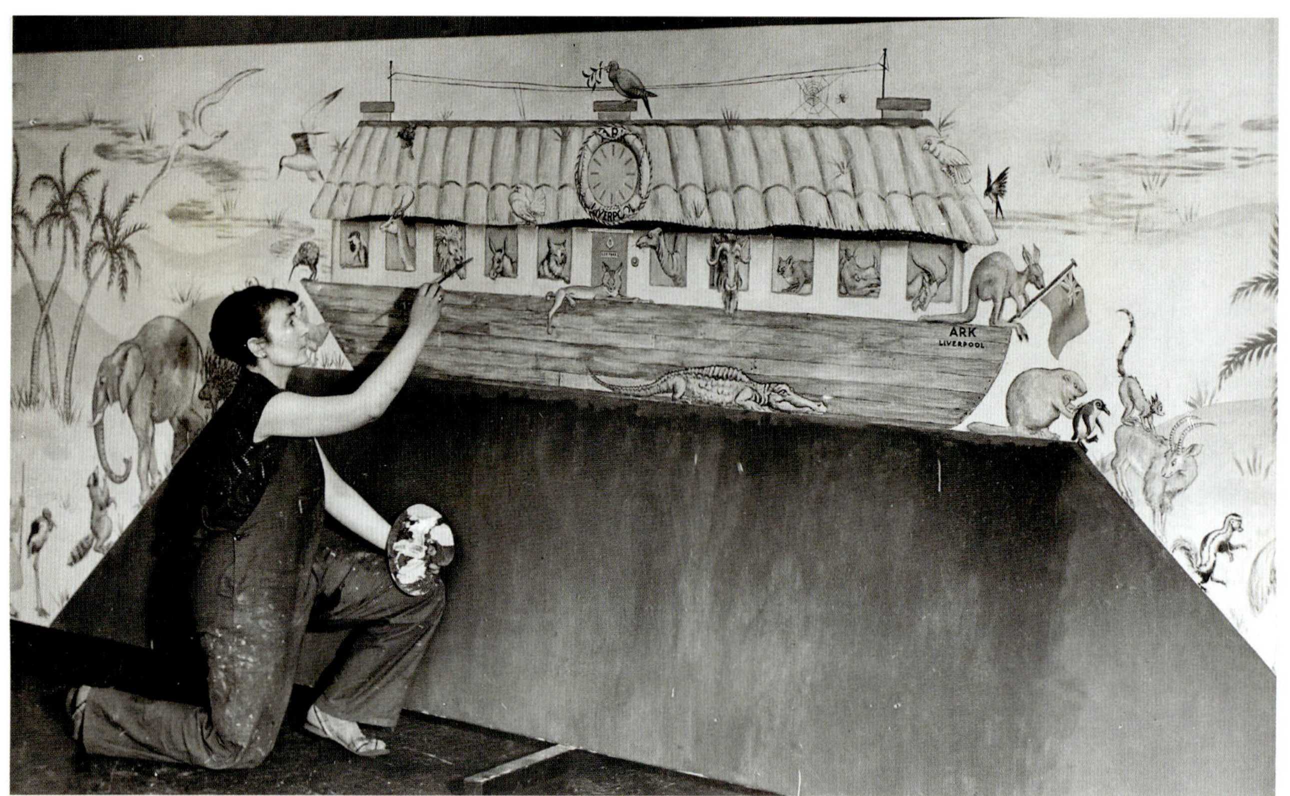

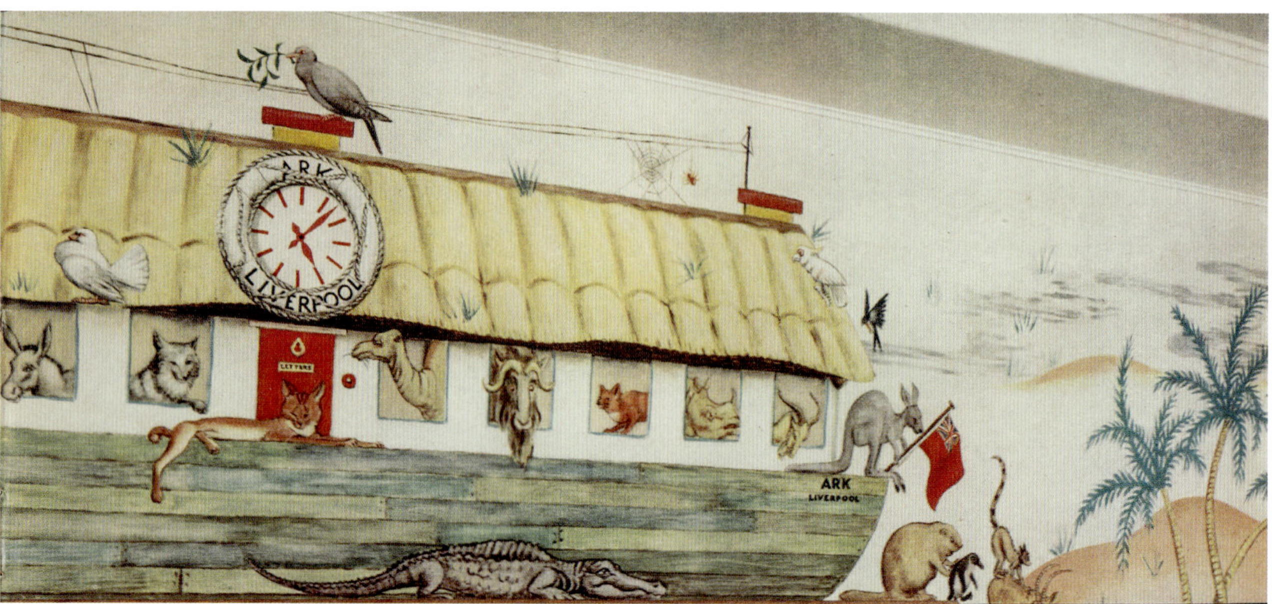

Less often mentioned is Herry's second piece for the ship: a map of Atlantic shipping routes, painted on metal, in the Tourist Class Smoking Room. A photograph of it was included in the September 1937 issue of *The Artist* magazine in an article by James Gardner entitled 'The Decorative Map as Advertisement'. It was also referred to in the *Gloucester Citizen* on 20 February 1936. This map mural was on nothing like the scale of the magnificent one by MacDonald Gill, *Map of the North Atlantic* (oil on wood), in the First-Class Dining Room, but was still impressive, with a compass and some good heraldry. The liner is now a tourist attraction at Long Beach in California.

Below: The Second-class (Tourist) Children's Playroom on R.M.S. *Queen Mary* showing Herry Perry's mural and the toys she made for the Playroom

Opposite top: Herry Perry painting her mural of Noah's ark for R.M.S. *Queen Mary* in late 1935/early 1936 (© Getty Images)

Opposite bottom: Part of Herry Perry's mural of Noah's ark on R.M.S. *Queen Mary*

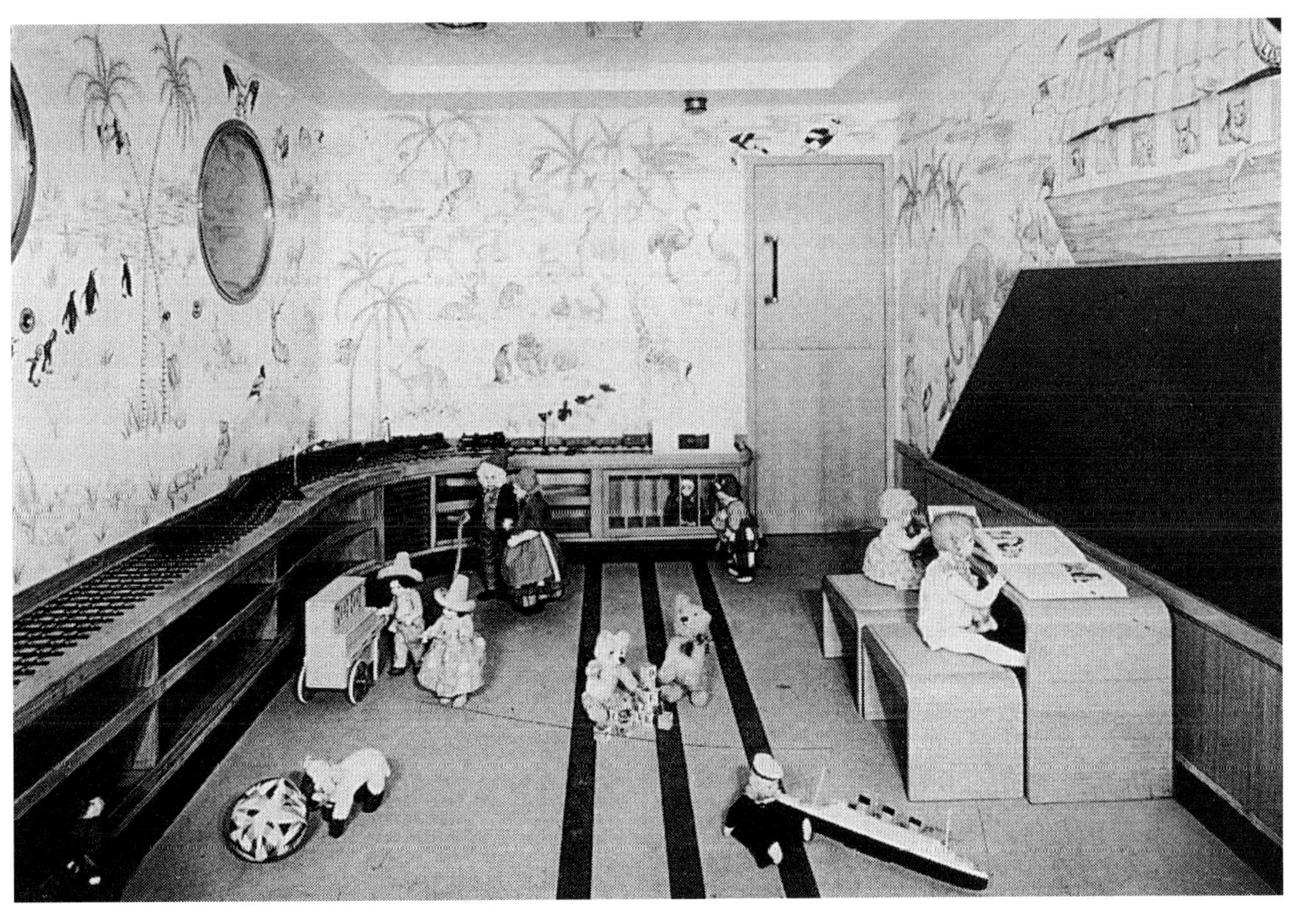

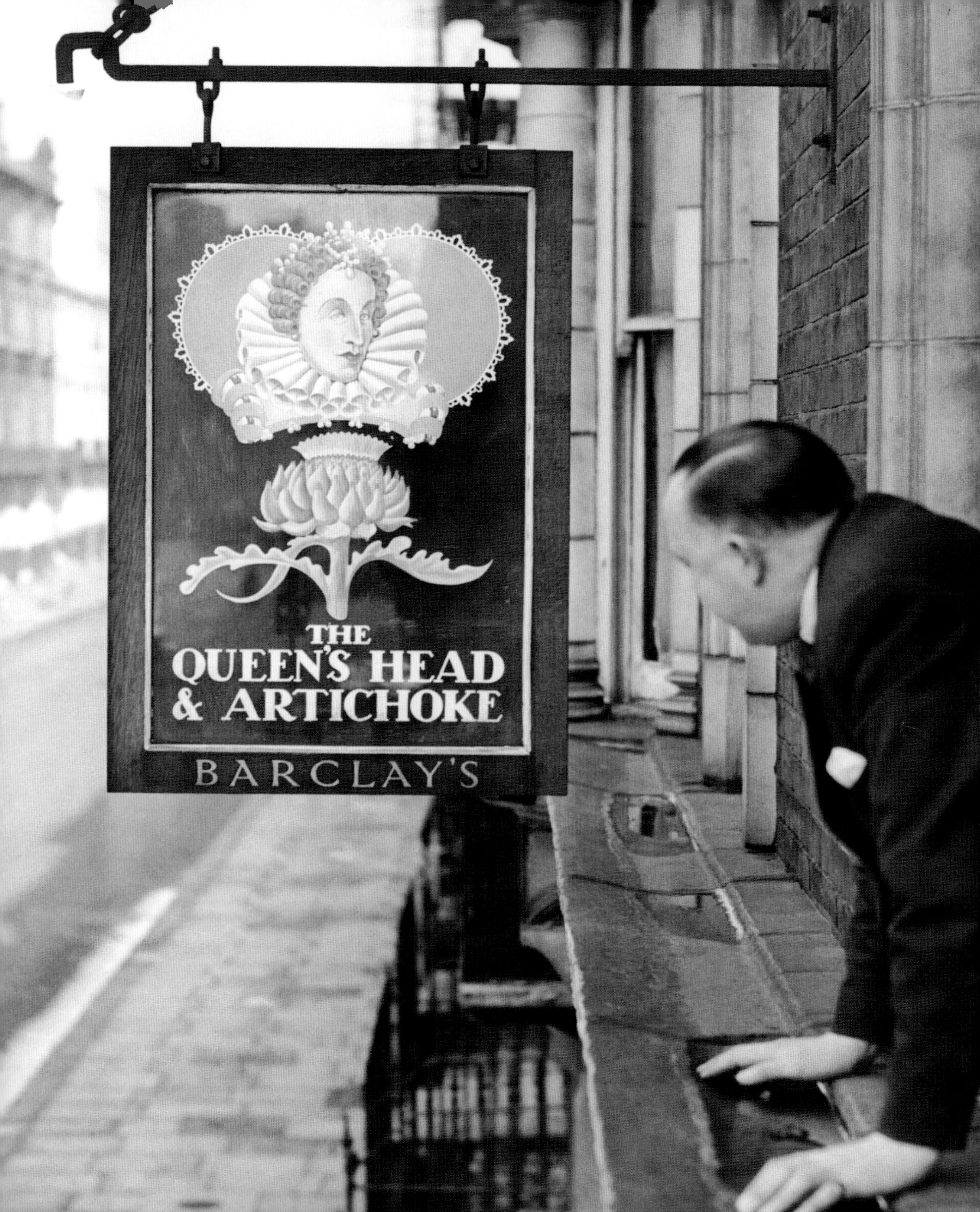

THE
QUEEN'S HEAD
& ARTICHOKE
BARCLAY'S

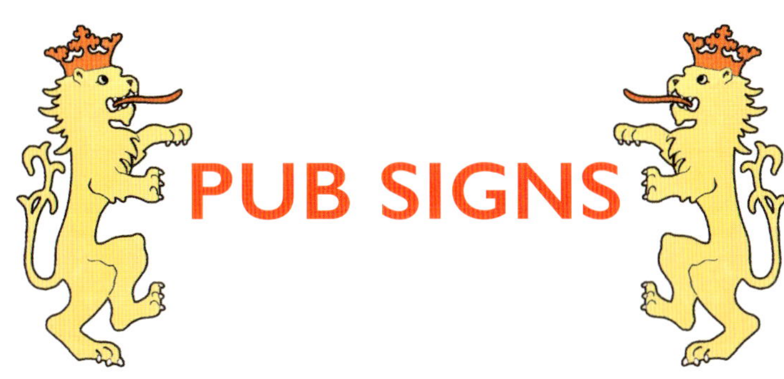

PUB SIGNS

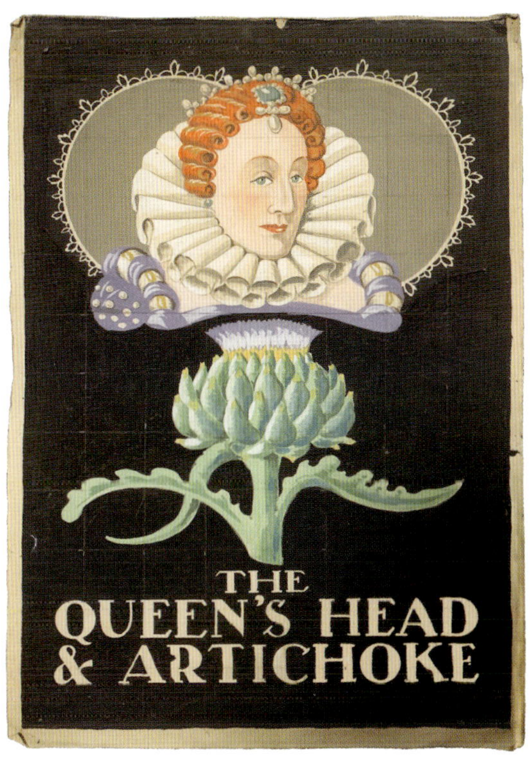

Above: The preparatory drawing for *The Queen's Head & Artichoke*, 1950s

Opposite: The newly installed pub sign for *The Queen's Head & Artichoke* in Albany Street, London NW1. Photograph by Roy Speller (© Getty Images), 1950s

In the 1950s, Herry produced a large number of pub signs for Barclay's, a London brewery (and then for Courage after it took over Barclay's in 1955), Friary Mieux, a Guildford brewery, and perhaps other breweries too. This was a period when breweries commissioned artists to paint their pub signs – Rachel Reckitt (1908–1995) was another artist who did this work. It's not known exactly how many signs Herry did, but we know of some 95 preparatory drawings, owned by the family, and there are also some photographs of the actual pub signs, taken in the 1950s. In one case, *The Queen's Head & Artichoke* in Albany Street, London NW1, we have both the artwork cartoon and a photograph. Many of the signs are amusing (*The Jolly Butchers* for example; and is the title animal in *The Reindeer* grinning?). She sometimes makes interesting choices for the signs: using a Phoenix moth for *The Phoenix* instead of the mythical bird, a chimney sweep for *The Black Boy* and a World War Two pilot for *The Happy Landing*. Some of the locations of the pubs photographed, or those with peculiar names, can be identified. It appears that none of the signs are currently on the pubs that have survived; some of the pubs were demolished or damaged during the Blitz and others were remodelled over the years.

Another source regarding the pub signs is Bill Pearson, a writer from New Zealand who was a lodger with Herry for three years from 1950 in her flat at 160a Haverstock Hill, London NW3. He served as a model for her signs for *The Hearts of Oak* in Dock Street, London E1, and *The Load of Hay* on Haverstock Hill. She also painted a portrait of him, in oil paint, in 1952. He described her as 'sociable and kind-natured' but 'rather possessive' (in Millar's book about him; see Selected Bibliography).

The pub signs also show Herry's interest in heraldry (which she may have inherited from her father; see 'Brief Biography'): a number of them feature coats of arms. These signs were expertly done by her. The family believe that she worked for the College of Arms in London designing coats of arms, but the College can find no evidence that she was employed by them or by individual Officers of Arms.

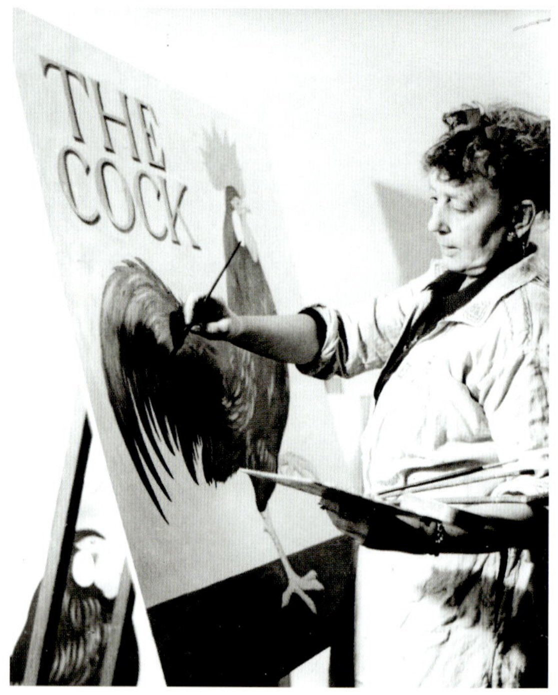

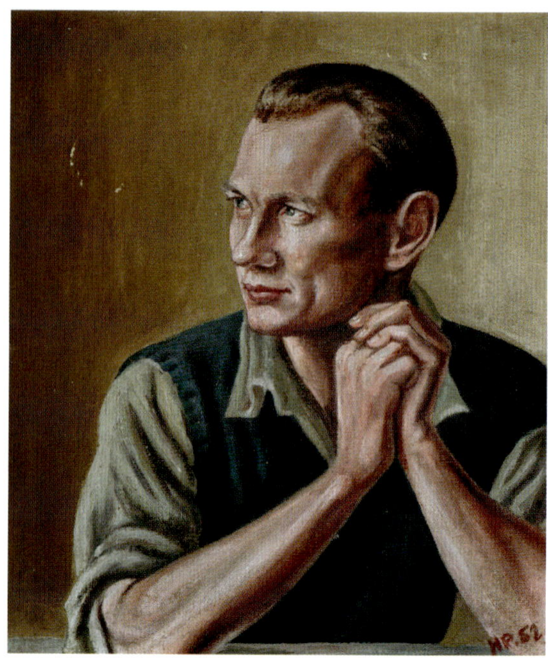

Top: Herry Perry painting a sign for *The Cock* pub, 1950s

Above: Portrait of Bill Pearson, oil on board, 1952 (courtesy of Alexander Turnball Library, Wellington, New Zealand ref. G-407)

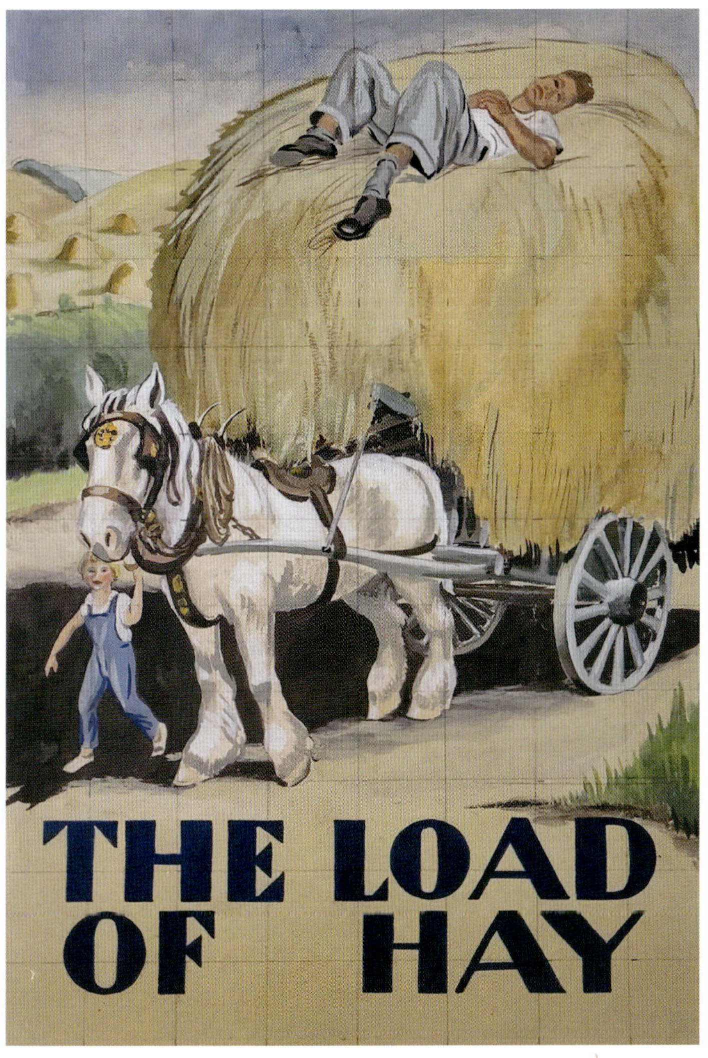

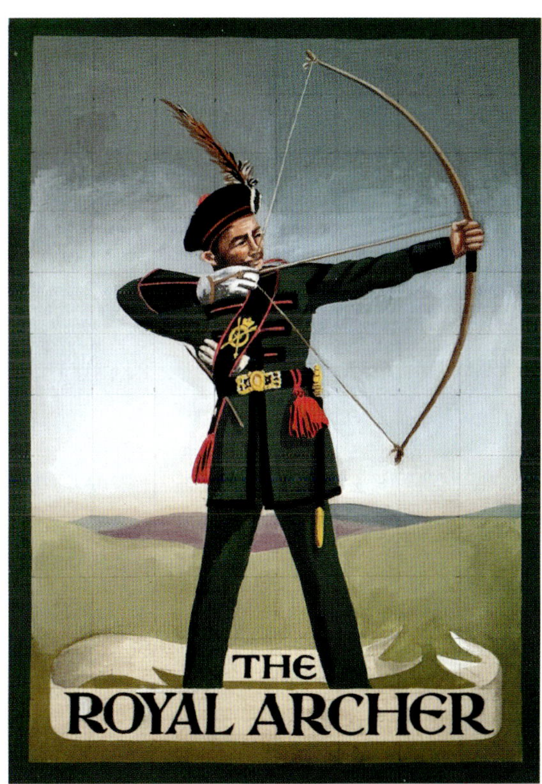

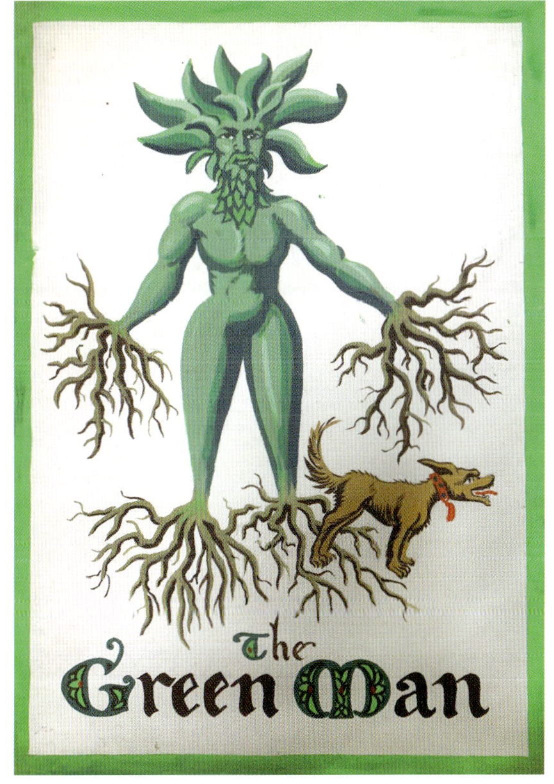

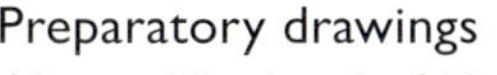
Preparatory drawings
Above: *The Load of Hay*, 1950s

Top right: *The Royal Archer*, 1950s

Bottom right: *The Green Man*, 1950s

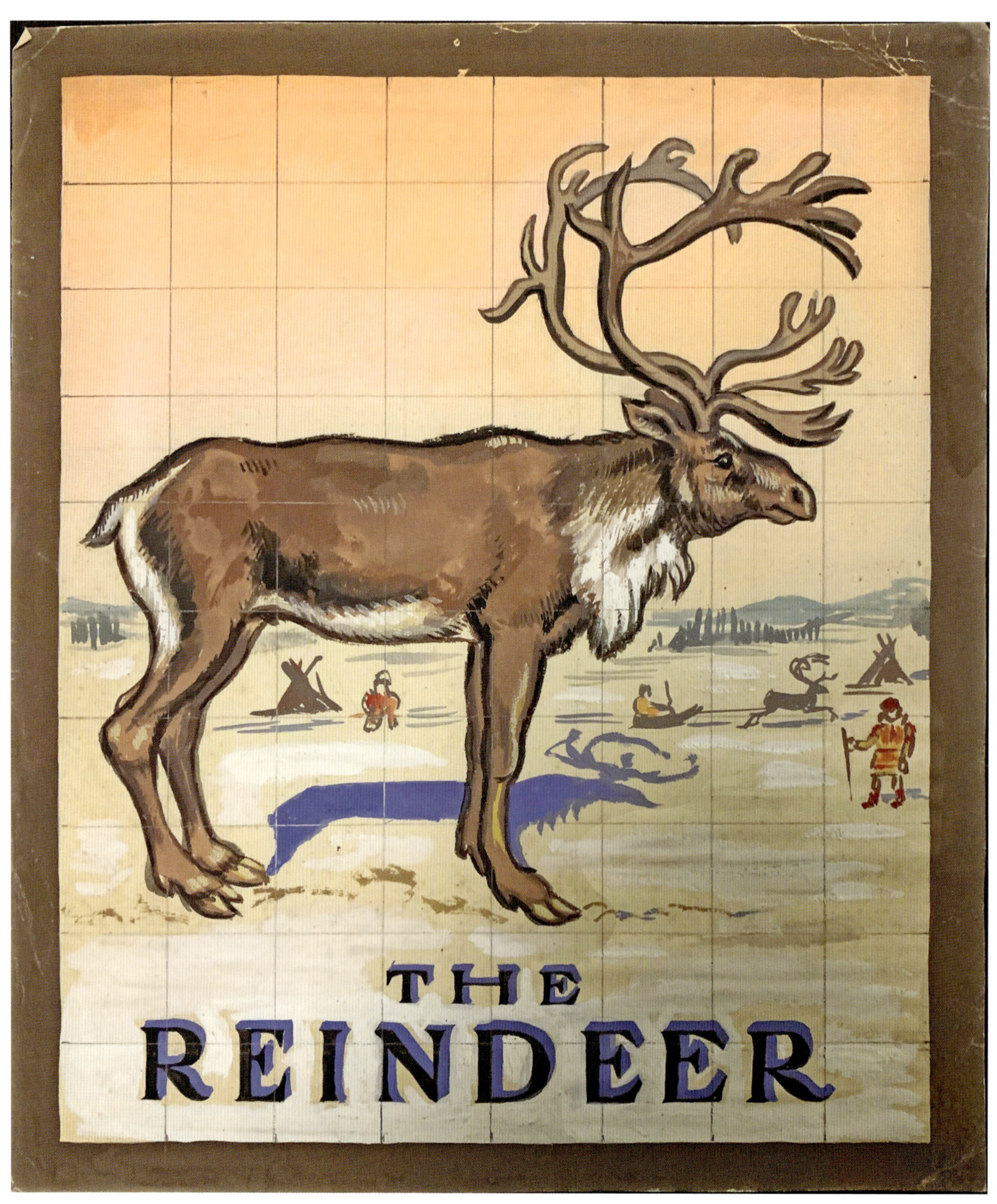

THE
REINDEER

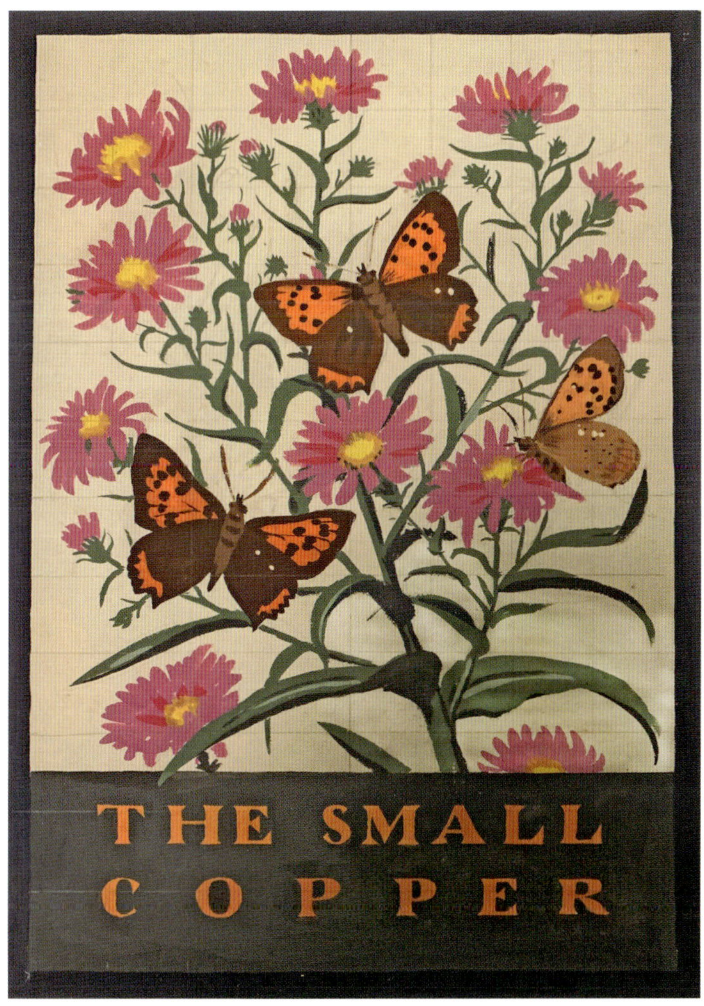

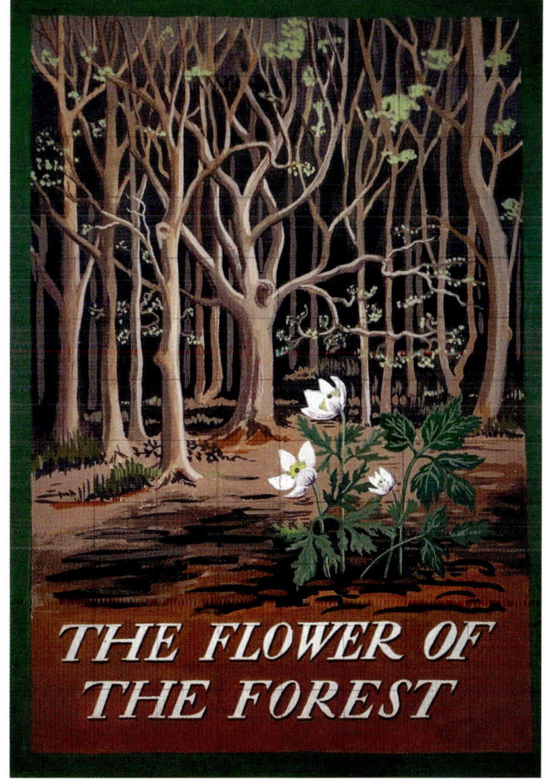

Preparatory drawings
Above: *The Small Copper*, 1950s

Top right: *Thicket Hotel*, 1950s

Bottom right: *The Flower Of The Forest*, 1950s

Opposite: *The Reindeer*, 1950s

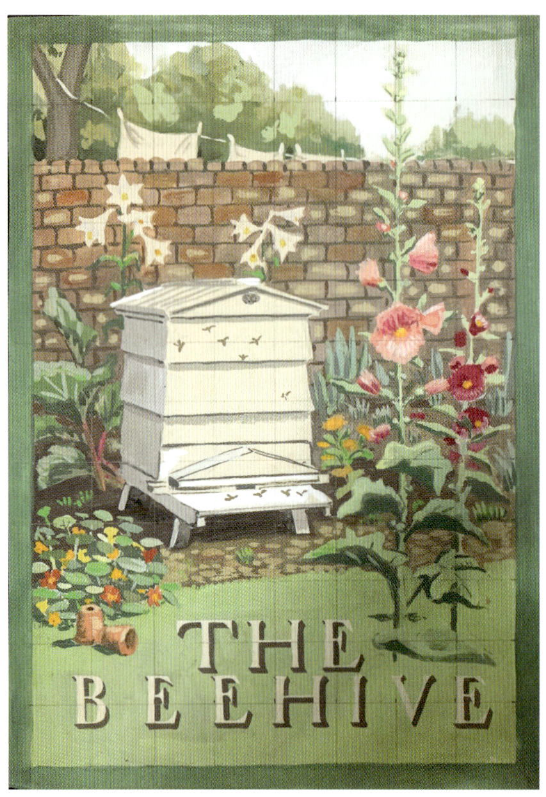

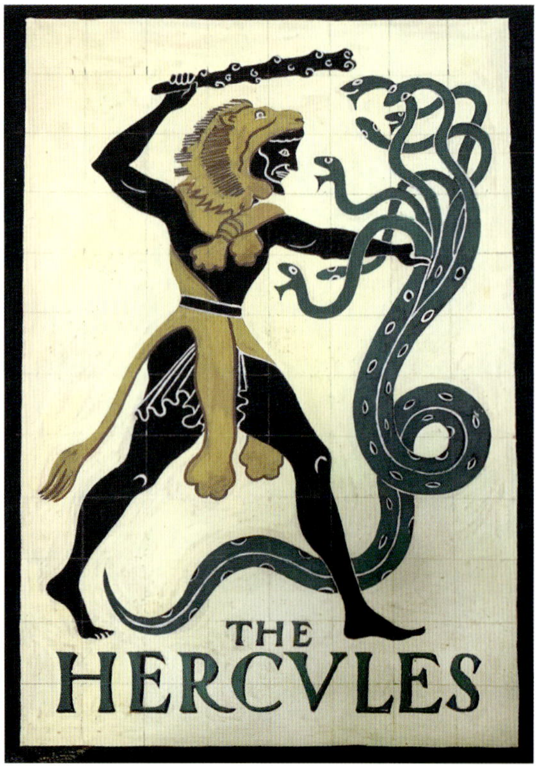

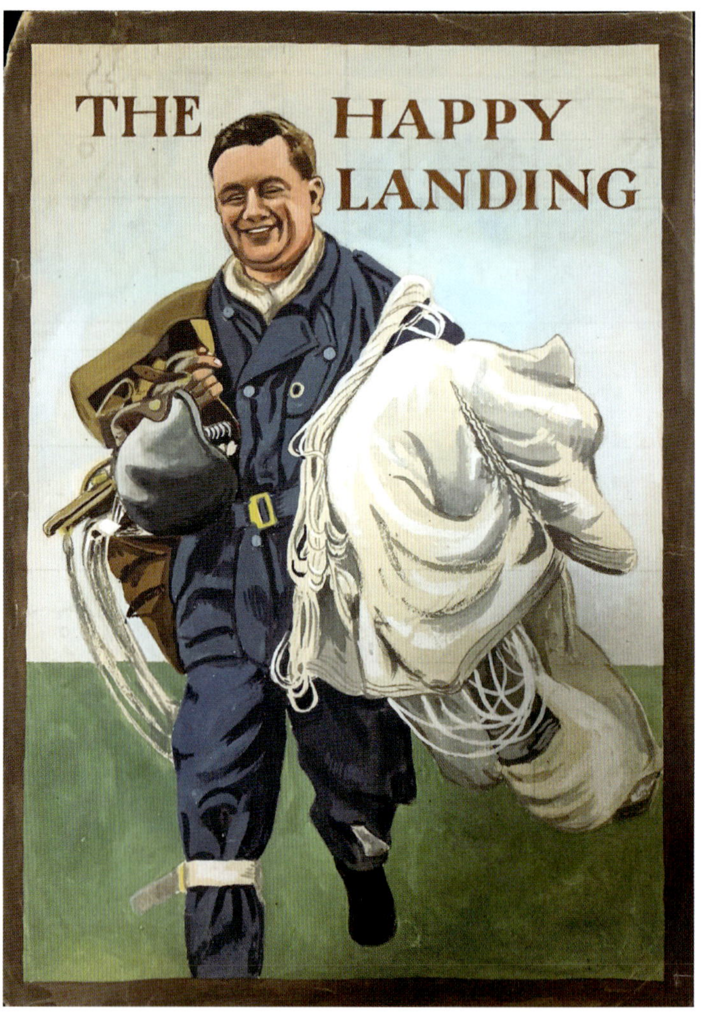

Preparatory drawings

Top left: *The Beehive*, 1950s

Top right: *The Happy Landing*, 1950s

Bottom left: *The Hercules*, 1950s

Opposite: *The Jolly Butchers*, 1950s

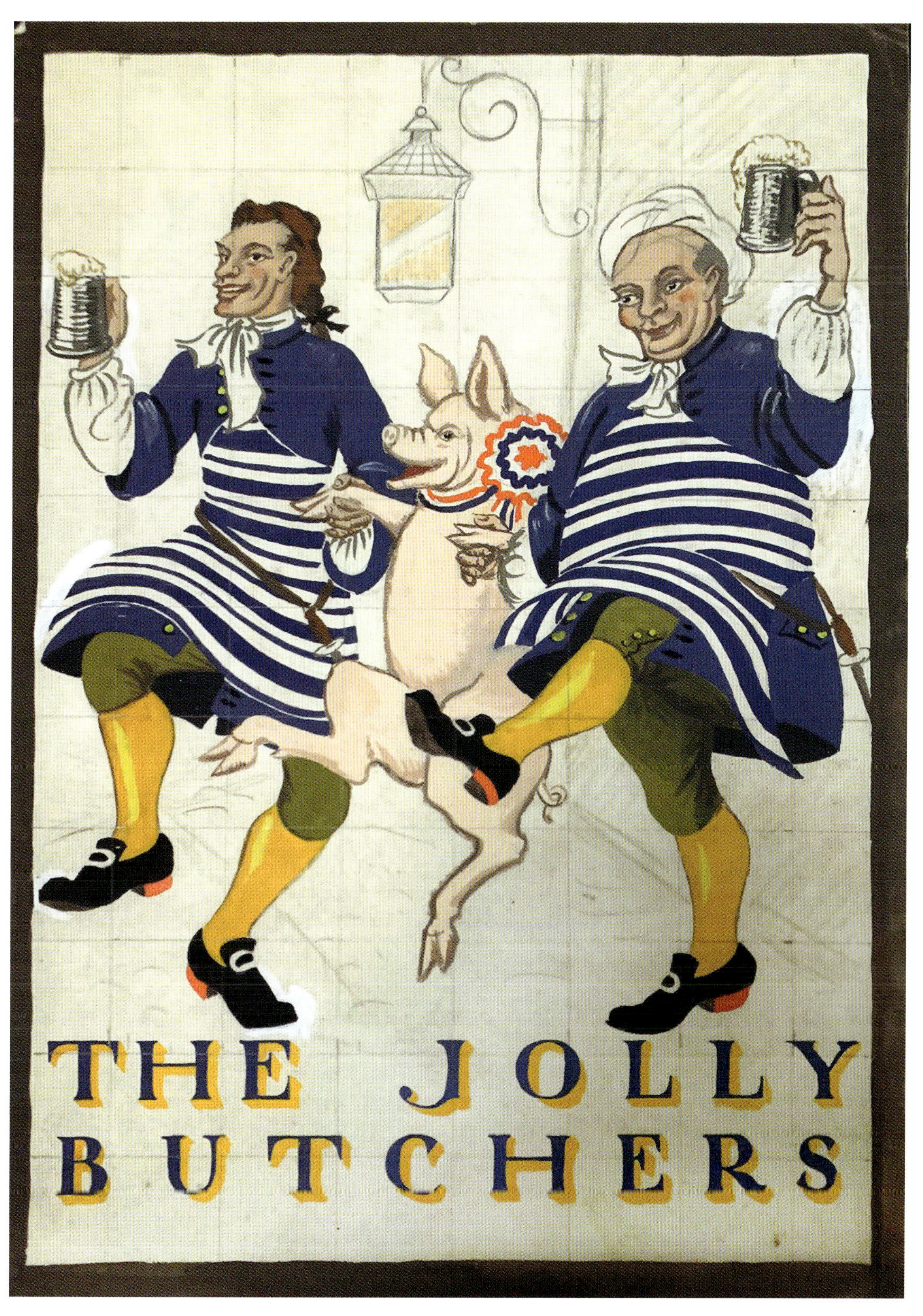

THE JOLLY
BUTCHERS

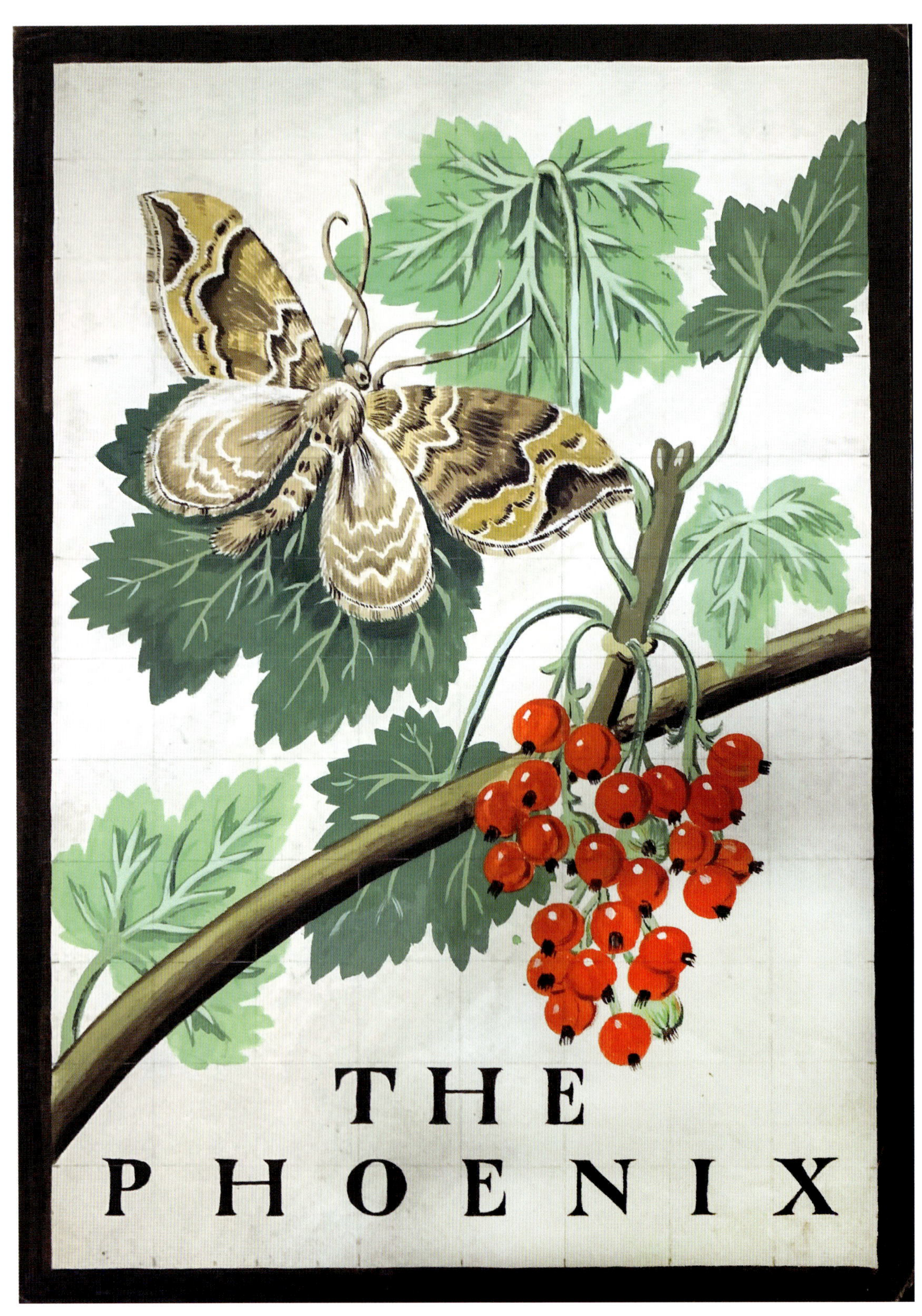
THE
PHOENIX

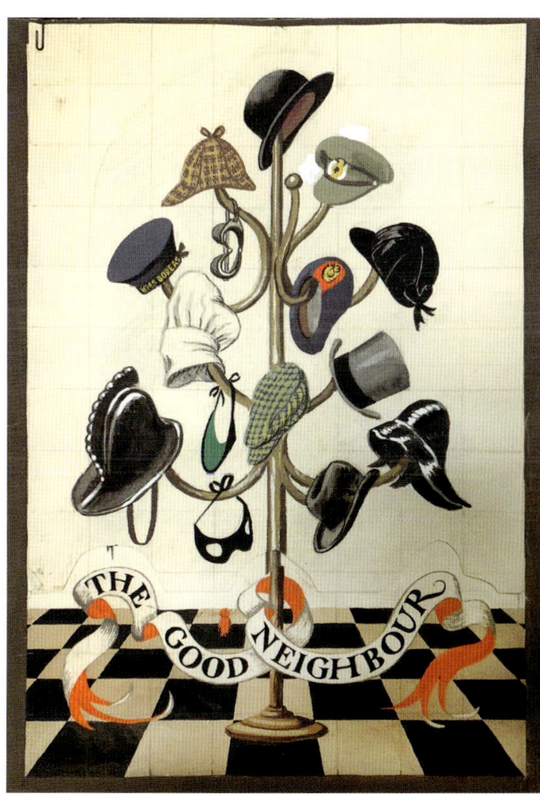

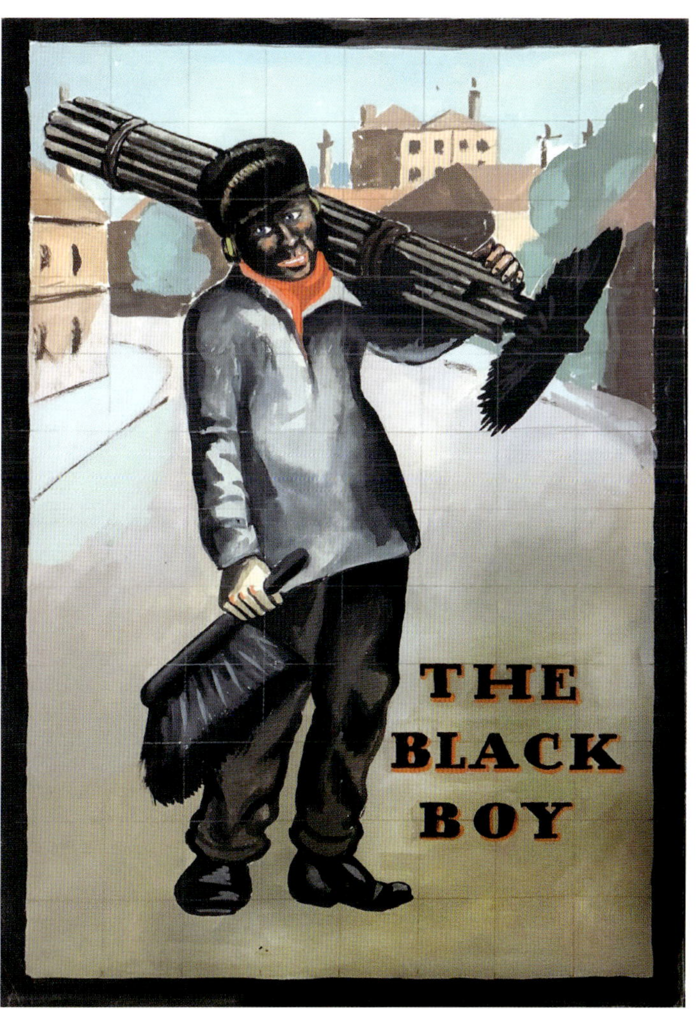

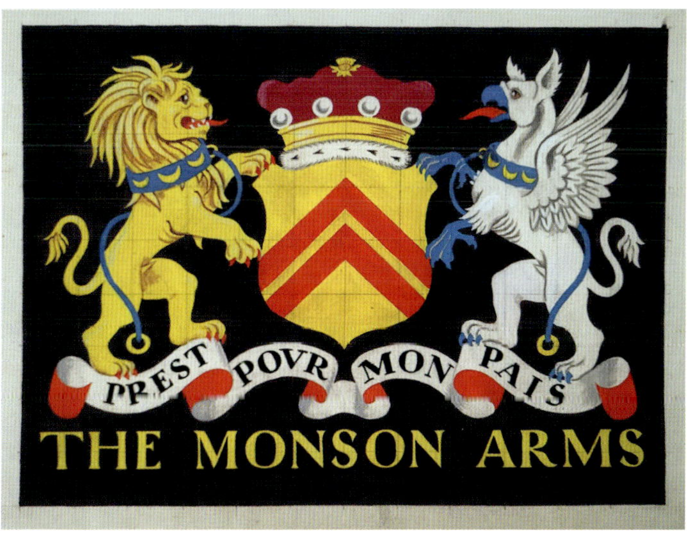

Preparatory drawings
Above: *The Good Neighbour*, 1950s
Top right: *The Black Boy*, 1950s
Bottom right: *The Monson Arms*, 1950s
Opposite: *The Phoenix*, 1950s

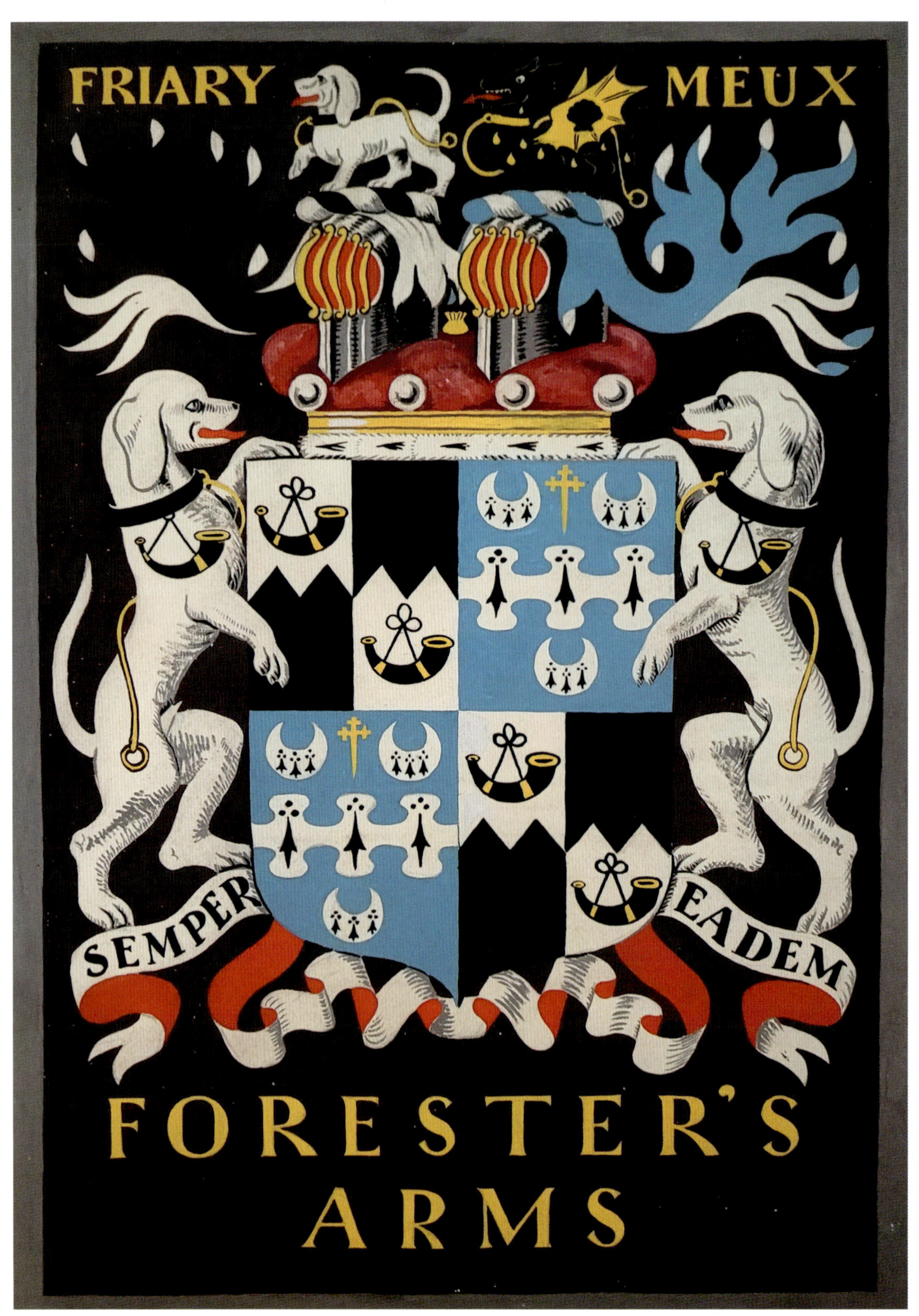

FRIARY
MEUX
SEMPER
EADEM
FORESTER'S
ARMS

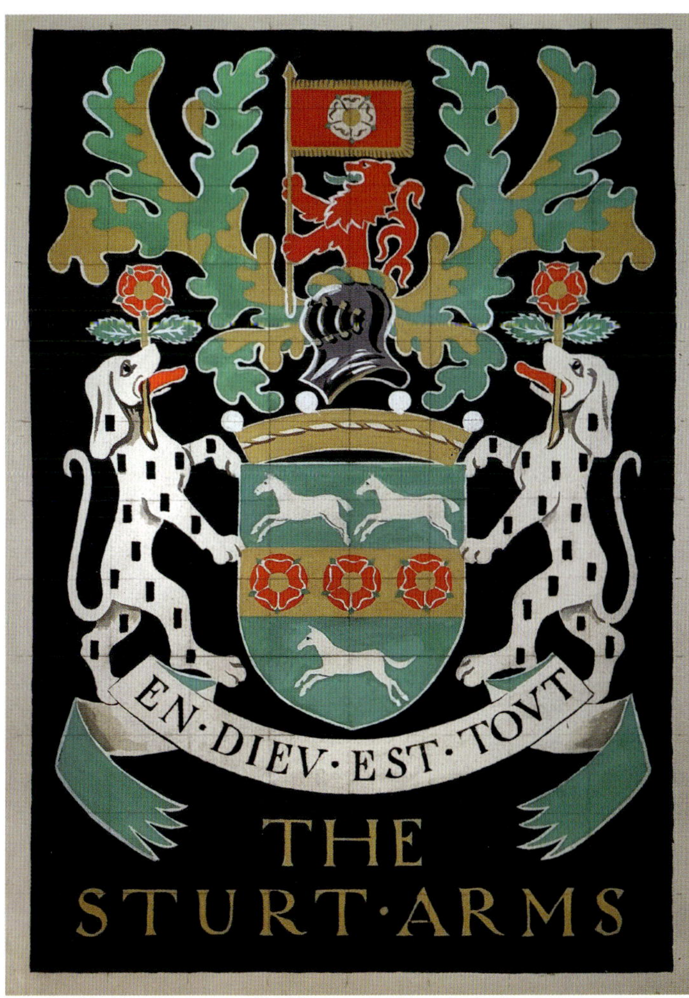

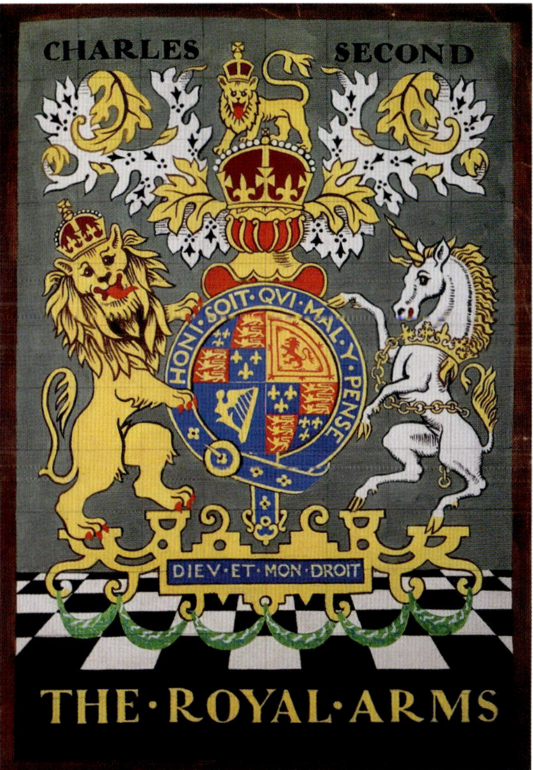

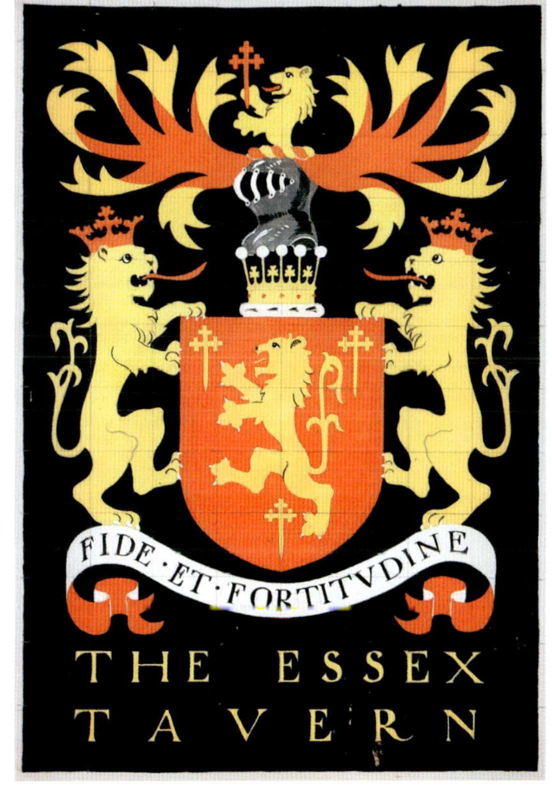

Preparatory drawings

Above: *The Sturt Arms,* 1950s

Top right: *The Royal Arms,* 1950s

Bottom right: *The Essex Tavern,* 1950s

Opposite: *Forester's Arms,* 1950s

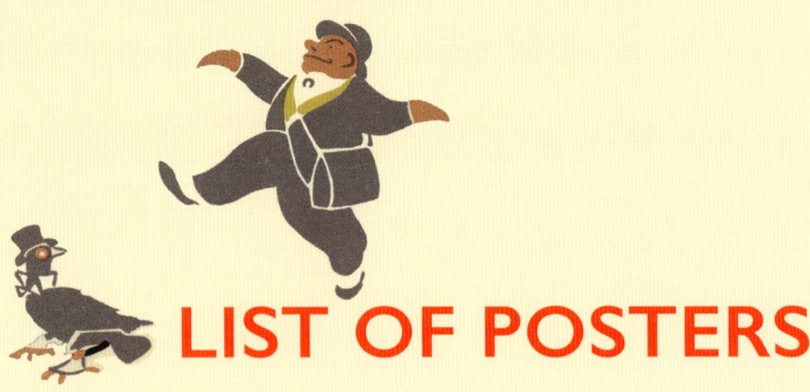

LIST OF POSTERS

All the posters below were designed for London Transport unless otherwise stated. Most of the London Transport posters (and some of the original artwork) can be found on the London Transport Museum website, www.ltmuseum.co.uk. A number next to a poster indicates where it can be found in this book.

1927
- The Empire under One Roof **(44)**
- A New Chart of the Royal Zoological Society's Gardens in Regent's Park **(45)**

1928
- Derby Day **(47)**
- The Zoo Alphabet **(46)**

1929
- Derby Day – St Dunstan's Coach Service (for St Dunstan's) **(frontispiece)**
- Morden
- Kew **(48/49)**
- South Harrow
- Hounslow
- Edgware
- London Thou Art the Flower of Cities All (for Great Western Railway) **(50/51)**

1930
- Country Joys from Golders Green Station
- Country Joys from Victoria Station
- Country Joys from Monument Station **(52)**
- Country Joys from Ealing Common Station
- Country Joys from Camden Town Station
- Country Joys from Morden Station
- Country Joys from Hounslow East Station
- Australia v. M.C.C. at Lord's

1931
- Blackberry Time **(56)**
- Bluebell Time
- Crocus Time
- Chestnut Sunday, Bushy Park
- Trooping the Colour
- Olympia International Horse Show
- R.A.F. Display
- Wimbledon **(57)**
- The Royal Tournament at Olympia
- Richmond Horse Show
- Derby Day – Book Your Bus or Coach Now **(58)**
- Derby Day – Buses Every 30 Seconds to the Course
- Motor Cycle and Cycle Show
- Cup Final
- Rugby Northern Union Cup Final **(59)**

1933
• Orpheus at Whipsnade
• Rugby League Cup Final **(59)**

1934
• 800 Miles of Rambles **(60)**
• The Theatres **(60)**
• Sight Seeing
• Visiting Friends
• It's Bank Holiday
• Dining Out
• Whitsun in the Country

1935
• Crocus Time
• Bluebell Time
• Chestnut Sunday, Bushy Park
• Whitsun in the Country
• Pleasure Outings
• Cup Final **(62)**
• Motor Show, Olympia
• Trooping the Colour
• Derby Day **(61)**
• Lord's England v. South Africa
• Wimbledon
• Richmond Royal Horse Show
• The Royal Tournament
• Lord Mayor's Show **(61)**
• Boat Race **(63)**
• Rugby League Final
• International Horse Show, Olympia **(64)**

1936
• Sports Clubs
• Parties

1937
• Cruft's Dog Show

1938
• Bertram Mills Circus **(65)**

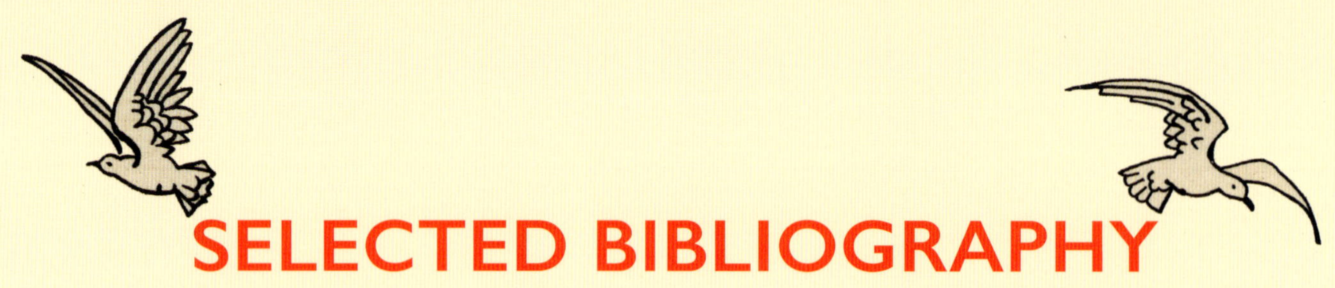

SELECTED BIBLIOGRAPHY

Wood Engraving, Sculpture and 'Stupid Little Jobs'
Lawrence, S., *Spitsticks and Multiples: The Society of Wood Engravers, 1920–46, and the English Wood Engraving Society*, The Fleece Press, Upper Denby, 2022

Maps and Posters
Artmonsky, R., *Designing Women: Women Working in Advertising and Publicity from the 1920s to the 1960s*, Artmonsky Arts, London, 2012

Bownes, D., *Poster Girls*, London Transport Museum, London, 2017

Bownes, D., and Green O., (eds), *London Transport Posters: A Century of Art and Design*, Lund Humphries, Aldershot, 2008

A Centenary Exhibition of London Transport Posters, exh. cat., Royal Institute Galleries, London, 2–30 July 1963

Green, O., *Underground Art*, Lawrence King Publishing, London, 1990

London Transport Museum website, at www.ltmuseum.co.uk

Walker, C., *MacDonald Gill: Charting a Life*, Unicorn, London, 2020

Murals

Hinkey, D.M., *The Art of the RMS Queen Mary*, Robert Gumbiner Foundation and Hippodrome Galleries of FHP Healthcare, Long Beach, CA, 1994

Liss, P., and S. Llewellyn (eds), *British Murals and Decorative Painting 1920–1960*, Sansom & Co, Bristol, 2013 (published to accompany the exhibition of the same name, 14 February–9 March 2013 at the Fine Art Society, London)

[no author] R.M.S. *Queen Mary*, Cunard White Star, London, 1936

Pub Signs

Bishop, H., *Rachel Reckitt: Where Everything That Meets the Eye … A Retrospective*, Somerset County Museums Service and the Golsoncott Foundation, 2001 (Published to accompany the exhibitions 'Paintings, works on paper' and 'Sculptures, works in the round' 18th August-13th October 2001, and 'All works' 20th October-30th November 2001, held at at Somerset County Museum, Somerset Rural Life Museum and the Royal Albert Memorial Museum)

Millar, P., *No Fretful Sleeper: A Life of Bill Pearson*, Auckland University Press, Auckland, 2010

INDEX

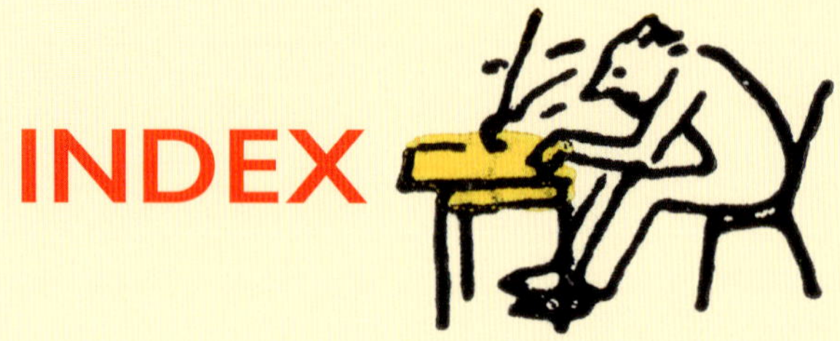

ACKNOWLEDGEMENTS

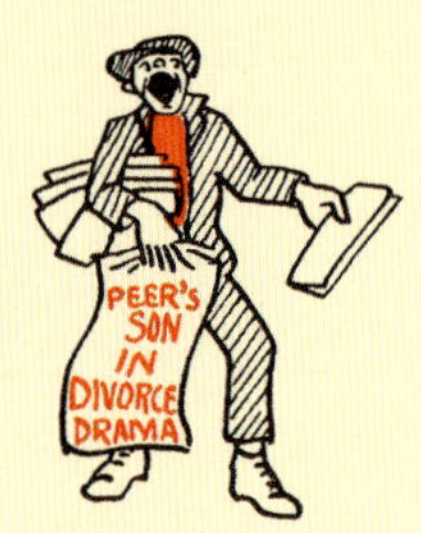

This book would not have been possible without the help of Herry Perry's nieces Libby Colterjohn and Judy Dunster. They and their families have sent me many pieces of her artwork and photographs of her, and Libby and Judy have shared their memories of their aunt with me. I am also indebted to Rod Barron for all his research about Herry in 2017, which has made my job much easier, and for his enthusiastic help with the book and particularly the sections on Maps and Posters and on Murals. I'm grateful to Simon Lawrence for putting me in touch with Libby and Judy and for helping me with some of the illustrations.

Thanks also to Anna Buruma for giving me access to the archives of Central Saint Martins and their collection of Herry's wood engravings, and to Debbie Barnes for allowing me access to the London Transport Museum archives and their collection of Herry's posters (and to Caterina Tiezzi for helping me with the poster images). I spent a very enjoyable day at Rothamsted Research with Catherine Fearnhead, Roger Plumb and John Jenkyn, and many thanks to them for all their information about the mural there as well as showing me other artwork by Herry and copying all the correspondence between Sir John Russell and Herry for me. Thanks also to Clara Frota of the Alexander Turnball Library, Wellington, New Zealand for help with material relating to Bill Pearson.

Particular thanks to Katy Mugford, who is even more of a Herry Perry fan than I am, for helping me in lots of ways to write the book. And to Katy and Richard Keenan for designing the book. Finally to Clara Hudson of Sansom & Co and Ann Kay for making the publication process so enjoyable and to John Hammond for his excellent photography.

This book was completed on the eve of 22 July 2024, the
Saint's Day of Mary Magdalene who had seven devils cast
out from her. It was seven devils of a job to get this book
about the bohemian, funny and ever observant
Herry Perry finished on time.

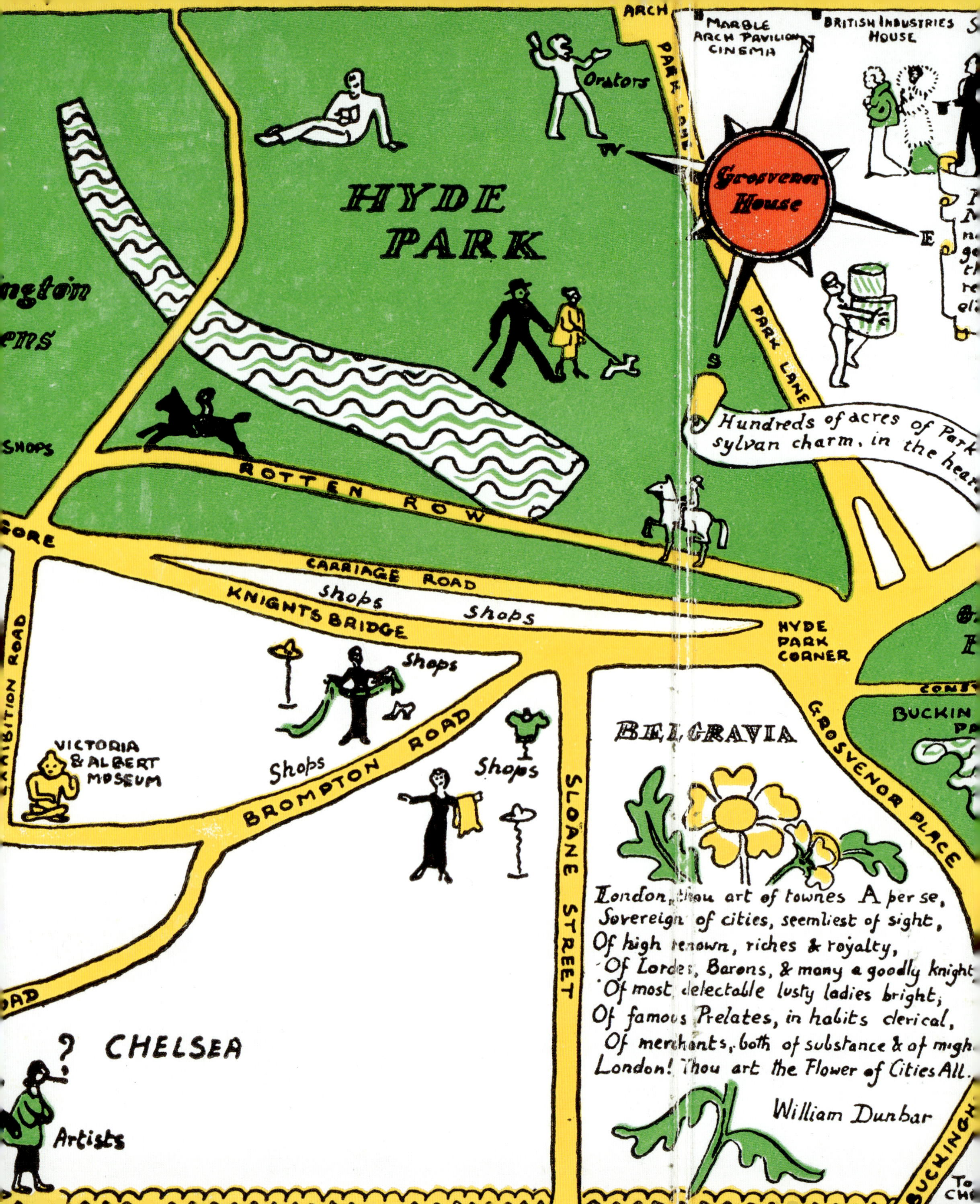

ARCH
MARBLE
ARCH PAVILION
CINEMA
BRITISH INDUSTRIES
HOUSE
Orators
HYDE
PARK
PARK LANE
W
S
E
Grosvenor
House
Hundreds of acres of Park
sylvan charm, in the hear
ROTTEN ROW
CARRIAGE ROAD
Shops   Shops
KNIGHTSBRIDGE
Shops
HYDE
PARK
CORNER
GROSVENOR PLACE
CONS
BUCKIN
PA
Shops
BROMPTON ROAD
Shops
VICTORIA
& ALBERT
MUSEUM
EXHIBITION ROAD
BELGRAVIA
SLOANE STREET
London, thou art of townes A per se,
Sovereign of cities, seemliest of sight,
Of high renown, riches & royalty,
Of Lordes, Barons, & many a goodly knight
Of most delectable lusty ladies bright,
Of famous Prelates, in habits clerical,
Of merchants, both of substance & of migh
London! Thou art the Flower of Cities All.

William Dunbar
? CHELSEA
Artists
BUCKIN